The Student Body
Student Ministry in Spiritual Alignment

glenn walters

www.xulonpress.com

special thanks

I would like to say thanks to my best friend, girlfriend, babies' momma, and wife, Emily. Thank you for your patience and understanding during this entire process. I know to a degree what being pregnant feels like (minus water weight gain, epidurals, and the whole birth canal experience) You have given me the space to grow and allow this book to develop full term in me. I love you now more than I thought possible on the day we exchanged vows.

To my best buddy and best baby girl, you had to endure a vacation with me physically present on the trip but not in the experience with you. Thank you for your indulgence. Noah, God promised me you would double my ministry. I can't wait to read your 2nd book. Kendy, thank you for the back rubs & drink refills while I typed all day. Your gift of hospitality is being displayed even today, at the age of six.

To my Head, Pastor Kemp, thank you for being a spiritual father of great integrity. We have been going at this well over a decade, and you are as much of a man of integrity today, as from the beginning. Thank you. I hear what fellow student pastors face, and I am grateful for you every day.

To my FMCOG church staff, both past and present, thank you for keeping me sharp. The Bible says, "Iron sharpens iron." This book is a testimony of what we have done to each other! Take that however you want too! Ha!

To my extended family, I love you. That's what's up.

To my student ministry staff & the shabbach staff, thank you for being flexible and committed to me and this journey. I know this isn't the end of our stretching, but we do have traction. Thank you for letting me lead you.

To the students of the FMCOG, both past and present, I love you and that's why I do what I do. I'm a "seed planter." I pray that a harvest is being produced in your life because of the position you have allowed me to hold. I long for the days when I can sit in my recliner, bald(er) and fat(er) and turn the TV on to watch you change the world!

To every pastor & leader who purchased this book for yourself or someone you love, thank you. Out of the millions of books you could have chosen, you gave me a shot. I am humbled and honored. My prayer is this book will prove to be a worthy investment of your money and time.

preface

It seems like only yesterday that a skinny, long-haired kid from East Coast Bible College came sniffing around the Fort Mill Church of God and our Student Ministries looking for an opportunity to serve and make a difference. The thing that finally got my attention was that he simply would not go away. In spite of a long distance to drive, attending college, and working to support a new wife, he kept serving and giving until eventually I came to see that this young man wasn't just talk - there was character, commitment and ability in him worth taking a chance on.

That was almost fifteen years ago and that "kid" (no longer skinny and the hair...well we'll not even go there) has matured into a man of God full of grace and truth who is an anointed voice of reason in this increasingly challenging world. I'm so glad I took that chance.

I'm referring of course to Glenn Walters. In a profession where "long-term" is counted in terms of months, Glenn has been my Student pastor for almost fifteen years. During that time I have witnessed the book you have in your hands being "fleshed out". The life-changing truths and practical applications that you will learn were not dredged up at leisure from the murky waters of the impassioned scholar. No, they came from the torrid, fast-paced waters of active, hands on, gut-wrenching, heart-breaking day-to-day ministry of a God-called Youth pastor. When you drink from this well of knowledge you will find life, refreshment and strength. I encourage you to drink deeply as you read and reread this powerful book and may God use it to minister to you and equip you that through your life and ministry the *"whole body will be joined and knit together...according to the effective working by which every part does its share to cause growth of the body for the edifying of itself in love"* (Ephesians 4:15-16).

David L. Kemp
Senior Pastor, Fort Mill Church of God

table of contents

Introduction

just so we're clear...

O n average, I read 12 -18 books a year. Those of you who know me may be extremely impressed. Most of you, however, are probably not impressed at all. Either way, let me give you a little insight into my personal life as a way to set up how invaluable this principle has become to me personally. And consequently also how important it is for you to get this principle that God has spent over a decade getting into me.

I hit a wall early in my ministry, and I could not grow anymore personally. This lack of personal growth became a cancer that quickly infected the numerical, spiritual, and discipleship growth of my student ministry. I found myself sick and tired of looking at the weary, burnt out faces of my teenagers. I had heard a speaker say once, "The pew is nothing more than a mirror of the platform.", and I did not like my reflection. I had pulled out all of my tricks. I had exhausted all of my games. My charisma and natural giftings could only take me so far, but I was not satisfied with where I had landed. I knew in my heart, and I had seen with my spiritual eyes, that I would accomplish so much more.

It was an extremely frustrating time in my life. I remember walking out of youth services week after week and collapsing into my brown leather recliner. I would glare past my 48" Flat screen TV and think of ways to overcome the barrier I was slamming into head-first. I would sit there slouching like a spineless jellyfish, casting blame on anybody I could point out other than myself. It wasn't long before I was envisioning ways to eliminate staff members that were lazy and unproductive. I visualized new ways to assassinate teenagers and put us all, parents and pastors alike, out of the misery those spawns of Satan had put us through. I even found myself trying to conjure up devious plans to slice the tires of Pastor's Jag and plant evidence that would incriminate the administrative pastor. All because I didn't get budgetary approval to buy the toys I thought were necessary to continue my success. I'm sure you want me to say, "Just kidding." I'm sorry, but I have to tell the truth and nothing but the truth so help me God.

After months of stagnate ministry, frustrating meetings, and a whole bunch of whining, I had to take a hard look at myself. My pastor says, "Any true leader is a consistent reader." I, however, assumed that my charisma and sarcastic jokes, accompanied by a biblical truth would be more than alluring for teens by the scores to beat down the doors of our youth facility. I assumed that with very little effort, all my staff would follow my lead, all the teen guys would want to be like me, and all the teen girls would want to marry a man just like me. If the Senior and Administrative Pastors would stay the heck out of my way, hundreds upon hundreds of teens would file in each week to see and hear the wonderful "Gospel according to Glenn" (aka: the GIV). Was I ever stupid!

I think that by working with teenagers day after day, you run the risk of them rubbing off on you as much as you on them. Like any normal, immature teenager, I found myself in rebellion and trying to push as many limits as possible. I was breaking rules and policies set into place by the God-Appointed leadership of the House where I was called to serve, always working with the motto "get forgiveness, not permission." And God help everybody in the line of fire if I did not get my way! I would do everything I could to punish those involved. I would throw myself on the floor and have a "temper-tantrum" until someone either let me have my way, or gave me some budget money to console me. The problem was that I was supposed to be the leader and not a teenager being led. Something had to change, and somehow I knew it was going to be me. It was only after I had exhausted all of me that realized I had to begin developing "me" in order to continue the growth and development of the teens God had chosen for me to lead.

As God always seems to do, He gave my pastor specific instructions on how to take our entire staff to another level. I was sitting in my normal seat with my normal folder and normal pen on what I thought was a normal Tuesday (this was before the iPad was introduced.) I was taking part in what I thought was a normal weekly staff meeting with a normal agenda. Was I ever wrong. So there we were, waiting to get started so we could get through it, get finished and get to lunch. Then Pastor walks into the room… with NO agenda. I know immediately, this is does not look good for our hero. He sits down in his seat and declares that God has shown him the next step in taking us, his staff, to another dimension of influence and affluence here at our church. (Brace yourself!) He says, "I feel as if God has asked me to require of you to read a minimum of 1 book per month and turn in a 2 page report on the content of the book and how it can effect change in your area in the next year."

Hold up! Let's do some math. That's twelve books this year… two pages per book… carry the 1… WHAT!?!? That means he wants twenty four, count 'em, 24 pages of book reports to be turned in this year! Are we going to be graded? Will we lose our recess time if we don't complete our home-work? Will he take away our snack after nap time? Does this guy realize I am a grown man who is entitled to make "grown man" decisions! That's it; my pastor has finally flipped his lid. Pad the walls. Sound the alarms. Get him the white jacket that straps in the back and helps him hug himself. Has anyone seen the little yellow bus that he escaped from?

He goes on to say, "if there are issues with my new requirement, I will be more than happy to accept your resignation." WHAT! Hey dude, I have a degree from Bible College! If you think for a minute that I paid $30,000 for an education just to go back to middle school and do book reports, you can forget it. Little did I know, God was starting me on a journey to learn the two mission critical principles I needed in order to achieve the Destiny that He had placed on my life.

Principle 1: Reading will give me new understanding and new perspectives much quicker than me discovering them through ignorant experiences of my own. To achieve success faster, learn from someone else's journey.

Principle 2: Spiritual alignment is a must in the student body. (This also happens to be the subject of the book you now hold in your hand.)

Maybe this book is a requirement from your Senior Pastor. Maybe it was on the sale rack or in the discount bin. Maybe you came across it at a seminar, worship service, or conference I was privileged to be at, and you thought you would give me a shot. Maybe someone sowed this book as a seed to grow fruit in your heart and life. Or maybe you just happened across it and something in you said, "Give this one your attention."

Whatever the chance meeting that brought you and this book together; please do not make this a "speed" read. "Why?" you ask.

What if I was to say, "You and your ministry can fulfill every purpose God has placed in you to fulfill?"

What if I was to say, "You can achieve every dream God has placed inside of you for your own personal life?"

What if I was so bold as to say, "Achieving those dreams and accomplishing those goals can be a relatively easy path to follow?"

What if I am the most arrogant author you have ever read because I say, "I can give you this one principle, explain how to fit this principle into your ministry structure, accompany it with a few applications and you will see a major shift in the unity of your student ministry and in the church where you are called to serve? The principle I am speaking of is that of Spiritual Authority, and successful application of this principle will quickly lead to growth spiritually, numerically, and in the discipling process of your teens."

Now, if you are a youth pastor of any caliber, I have just made you laugh or gotten you very interested in this principle that God has taught me through more than a decade of youth pastoring at the same local church. I pray it is the latter. Trust me, I know there are a ton of books out there by authors who have decades more experience than I do on this subject. But I feel God has assigned me to this task to bring the perspective of the Youth Pastor to light. I have many youth pastors that I mentor who struggle with this issue. I, myself, fought against this principle even though I knew it was my own pride and ignorance that was keeping me from the fullest blessing of God. It became especially clear I had issues in this area of my life when my pastor asked me to read 12 books a year and do book reports on each. Believe me, our Commander and Chief couldn't pass a law that would require me to do book reports, much less someone I could quit on and to find an easier position. But this issue was not about reading or liking to read. This issue in me was not even about knowing it all or knowing nothing. This was about my obedience. This was really about my submission. My submission that would in turn, give others under me the proper perspective on Kingdom living, not democratic debating.

I want to share with you God's principle of Spiritual Authority for Youth Pastors. I am convinced this book is a mandate for me. As I am typing this introduction, I can't help but laugh at how ironic it is for me to be writing a book. I have prided myself on knowing I read little to nothing throughout my academic career. The greatest triumph of my college years was to know just enough about the book to add a little charm and a lot of flattery to get a "get-by" grade. Unfortunately, sycophants and speed-talkers can't survive long-term in youth ministry; trust me I've seen my share of colleagues try. And I can't find anywhere in living a Christ-honoring life where "getting by" is the standard for success. My goal in this book is to inspire you, to encourage you, and in some cases, offend you into the next dimension of anointing, next level of blessing, and a place where uncommon favor easily flows into every area of your life. I want more than anything for you to prosper. I believe that this book, my mandate, will put the tools in your hand to set you, and all who are above you and beneath you, on a course for supernatural gifts to flow into you, your leader, your staff, your teens, and your teens that are on their way.

I feel the best way to illustrate this alignment structure is by using the human body as the Student Body's metaphor. It was the human body that the Father took the time to shape with His hands in the Garden. When Christ came to atone for the sin and shame of humanity, He wrapped Himself in the shell of a human body. I believe God's call is to every "Body" not just everyone. I believe He is searching today for the "SUM" of the Body, not just somebody.

In light of that, I feel it is necessary to take you through the Student Body structure by looking at it as a human body. No, I will not deal with zits, voice changes, and weird adolescent stages. I will, however, follow the head-to-toe structure the human body gives us. It is my desire for you to easily grasp this authority structure. That way, you can align properly the Student Body God has placed you in leadership of.

Additionally, I have placed bonus suggestions to help you along the way. Things I have learned, practices I have applied, and principles that may challenge you. I have categorized them in two specific ways.

The first way is what I call, **"I'm not fussing..."**

This statement is one of my catch-phrases. Youth pastors I mentor on a consistent basis, my staff (volunteer and paid), and even my teens all grin every time I start a conversation with these words. "I'm not fussing" are challenges for you. I have made many dumb decisions and seen some of my dearest friends in ministry make those same mistakes. I want to make sure I highlight in every chapter some piece of knowledge you can gain from my mistakes and hopefully avoid your own.

The second way is what I call, **"What you need to do..."**

I almost laughed out loud when I typed that. This statement is one of my biggest pet-peeves. I despise hearing someone make that statement to me more than I despise having a 24 hour lock-in. I hate that statement more than a 10 hour drive in a 15 passenger van with all teenage girls who have to "potty" every 7 ½ minutes. I loathe that statement more than walking up to one of my student leaders doing something absolutely stupid, and when I ask them what he or she is doing, their response is, "I don't know." This little section in each chapter is designed to spark some sort of creative thought in you. Some of "what you need to do...'s" goal will be to make you smile and relax, while others will try to get you thinking of ways to bring each of the groups we discuss into alignment and under authority to continue the flow of God's blessing, favor, and anointing.

I am not the guy who assumes everyone wants to read his words. As a matter of fact, I am sitting here at my desk with butterflies in my belly wondering if I am wasting my time. Is this some futile effort of mine? Knowing where I came from and knowing how inadequate I am right now, do I even risk wasting time writing a book when I could be spending it in my Student Body? But beside those butterflies in the pit of my stomach is a calm assurance that I wouldn't have this burning mandate if other student pastors did not need to know what God has spent almost a decade and a half teaching me. Let's you and I spend some time together getting your Student Body into alignment.

Chapter 1

It's a Flow Thing –
You Must Understand

"Go up to the land flowing..."
Exodus: 33:3

There is a prominent family in my church: the Smith family. They are a large family and are closely knit together as a family unit. And I don't mean just brothers and sisters. No, there are cousins, aunts, uncles, and 3rd / 4th generation cousins that are truly committed to one another. I am not portraying them as the model family. They would not appreciate the pressure. But I do admire the system in which the Smith family operates. They understand there is a structure of authority, and everyone falls in line. This even applies to their vehicles. The youngest son, John, in one branch of the Smith family turned 16 and received my favorite vehicle in the line of hand-me-downs. The 1994 white Ford Bronco. (Yes, it is almost identical to the one O.J. Simpson road around in after the murder of his wife. Is that weird of me? Yes, but it doesn't change the fact that I like the SUV.) This particular Ford Bronco started as Dad's work vehicle and passed through 3 other sons before coming into the hands of the youngest son, John. Of course John had been around that truck forever, and to this day it is still my favorite. It was not exactly what John wanted by any means for his 16th birthday, but it was the one he received. What I appreciate most is not that Dad didn't spoil his kids with material things, but that there was a system in which he operated. As a new vehicle came to the family, everyone got an upgrade. The father, Eddie, always bought and kept the newest vehicle for himself. He wouldn't trade in his old vehicle. He would keep it and hand it down to the oldest son who handed his vehicle to the second oldest who gave his to the 3rd oldest. So every one of the boys got a newer vehicle than the one they were driving before his new purchase. It was fun for me to watch this system in action. It was so unique to the affluent suburban community I serve in that the Smiths adopted a motto they placed on all of their vehicles. The motto was: "it's a Smith thing, you wouldn't understand." In other words, unless you are a part of this family system, you will never understand why we do what we do. This motto also leaves you with the impression they are okay with people on the outside not understanding. It also leaves you to assume they realize their system is not normal nor is it politically correct. And they are okay with that.

Well, I would like to play off their story and borrow a portion of their motto to say that this Spiritual Authority "thing" that God has set into place is a "Flow Thing", but you must understand. For your sake, you must understand. For your senior pastor's sake, you must understand. For your paid and volunteer staff's sake, you must understand. For your students' sake, you must understand. By understand, I do not mean to just be knowledgeable about it. I mean, you must understand where you do and where you do not fit. You must understand what roles you are to play and what roles you are not to play. You must understand where your staff fits and the tools and objectives necessary for them to fulfill their roles. You must understand where your teens fit and also how to break them into components that compliment their respective stages of spiritual growth. Why? It's a "flow thing." It is imperative for you, your staff, your students and your future students to have a structure in place that gets this "flow thing" to everyone. The "flow" only takes place when everyone, from head to toe, is in their position and functioning under authority in the Student Body.

The power of positioning

Have you ever witnessed a tee-ball game? It is hilarious to watch kids who are enthused about playing a game in spite of the fact that they have no idea about the fundamentals. I recall last year when I went to watch my nephew Joshua play in his tee-ball game. It was utter chaos, but it was cute. When the ball was hit, everyone in the field who was interested in playing ran toward the ball. Right fielders would sprint across the field toward third base throwing their glove to the ground to get the ball. While others sat down to watch the birds fly above the field or do lawn manicures in the outfield. Those kids were absolutely clueless about the game going on around them, not to mention their strategic role to play in order for the team to be victorious. Now contrast that image to a professional baseball team. Everyone on the field knows exactly what is required of them. Everyone on the field operates as one unit to fulfill the team goal of victory. Everyone on the team understands their own strengths and weaknesses. Everyone on the team knows the strengths and weaknesses of their teammates. The team in turn brings that knowledge and their abilities together to balance each other and bring home the victory. Which description best fits the Student Body you have? Be real with yourself. Is your ministry a free-for-all? Do your staff, your students, and/or you float around chasing every new thing that pops into your field? Is it a collection of spiritually immature Christians star gazing and game playing on the same field? Do you have some of your ministry volunteer staff running around trying to play every position, while others do not even realize there is a game to win? Or is it a finely tuned, organized Student Body? Is it a Student Body where everyone knows their role, and will their role at this stage in their life, bring them the most satisfaction? For option 2 to become your reality, you need proper positioning. Once those who are a part of the Student Body are positioned, they must be given the training and the tools to fulfill their role.

Why is getting everyone in the right position so important? God is HUGE into positioning. From Adam all the way to modern day, God has been positioning from the very foundations of the earth. Let's use Joseph as the example of God strategically positioning one person to fulfill the God-given mandate on his life. Think about the "Dreamer" for a minute. Joseph is a dreamer and can interpret the dreams of others. He is an exceptional person with an exceptional destiny on his life. Imagine God plotting the course of your life and showing you what you'll be, while in your slumber. Now imagine he adds to it by using you to show others God's course for their lives. What an exceptional gift. Even more impressive to me is Joseph's ability to use that gift to find favor in all he goes through. Joseph knows what God has shown him. He understands that great destiny is on his life. He has even seen that he will one day have his own brothers kneeling before him. God mapped Joseph's life before the foundations of the earth. God knew He must set Joseph's life in such a way that He, alone, could get the glory for what He created Joseph to be. So, God positioned Joseph as the youngest son of Jacob. As youngest, he was entitled to the least of Jacob's inheritance. Yet, Joseph was favored by Jacob more than the other sons. Joseph was favored more than Rueben and even more than Judah. It was Joseph's positioning as Jacob's favorite that also positioned him as the object of hatred from his brothers. This was a horrible, yet necessary, place to be. It was this positioning that caused

Joseph to be <u>positioned</u> in the pit. Joseph was <u>positioned</u> in the pit at just the right time for the Midianites to come by and purchase him as a slave. It was because of his <u>position</u> as a slave with the Ishmaelites, that he was purchased by the captain of the guards, Potiphar, in Egypt. Joseph immediately found favor in the household of Potiphar. So much that Joseph began looking more like a member of the family than a member of the staff. Yet, this <u>positioning</u> put him in the <u>position</u> of choosing whether, or not, to sleep with his master's wife. Because he <u>positioned</u> himself in the place of good, moral character, he was then <u>positioned</u> in prison. While in this <u>position</u>, he began to find favor again. Using his gifts to show the waiter and the baker what God was showing them in their dreams, he <u>positioned</u> himself as a prospect for the king to use. Let me stop right here and encourage you to never hold back from using your gifts. Never, ever let the size of the crowd determine the amount you use your gift. I preach to a congregation of 12 just as hard as I do to a youth service of 200, just as hard as I do to a Sunday morning service of 1200, just as hard as I do to a youth conference of 3300. Why? 2 reasons:

1. I am not delivering MY words, so I can't deem this opportunity a waste of MY time. I have to believe that God has anointed me and appointed me to give His words to His people in His timing. Who am I to say the crowd isn't big enough for God to get His Word delivered?

2. You never know who is in the crowd. Yes, Joseph used his gift for only two. But it was those two that ran to give word to the king. It was those two that initiated his promotion to the next position. Don't ever hold back because of the size of the crowd. You never know who holds the key to your next promotion!

If Joseph had been the type of person who only uses his gift when the "numbers" were right, he would have missed the opportunity for his name to be mentioned before the king. It was Joseph's willingness to use his gift while being positioned in the prison that put him in position of being in front of the king. It is his position of running Egypt's food supply during the famine that gets his brothers on their knees in front of him. While Joseph is standing in his position, he sees God fulfill His purpose. Please understand, Joseph fulfilled his dream because he was submissive to the process.

To be in a position does not automatically put you in the front of the line for promotion. Joseph's success came because he was submissive to the process no matter what the position. Try and find anywhere through Joseph's process where he wasn't submissive. If ever a man had a reason to whine or defend himself, it was Joseph. How can a man live through all he lived through and still submit to the process? I found it in Genesis 39:2 "The LORD was with Joseph and he prospered..."

All throughout the Bible, I can give you examples of proper positioning. I have sat through countless testimonies of God taking people from a position of obscurity to a position of prosperity. There is an alignment that God has set in place to balance all those who follow His lordship.

Aaron's Anointing

I believe the balance that produces the proper attitude during God positioning us is found in Psalm 133.

Ps 133: 1 How good and pleasant it is when brothers live together in unity! 2 It is like precious oil poured on the head, running down on the beard, running down on Aaron's beard, down upon the collar of his robes. 3 It is as if the dew of Hermon were falling on Mount Zion. For there the LORD bestows his blessing, even life forevermore.

I know you're sitting there thinking, "That's it? I've heard that scripture all of my Christian existence." Yes, this is it! I'm sure you've heard this passage often. My question is not have you heard this passage, but have you seen this passage lived out? I am so tired of *hearing* about the miracles and the commanded blessing, I want to be a part of the church that *sees* the miracles and *lives* in the kind of unity that moves God to release the flow of blessing. I believe the significance of this passage has been missed for so long. This "flow thing" can only take place if we are positioned in UNITY. I know, I know, you get along with everyone. There is no static between you and your pastor. There is no static between you and the others on staff with you at the church. You and your youth staff are all on the same page. Your kids in your youth group even think you're the coolest dude in the county. And besides the little drama that happens each week between, "He said that you said that I said that she said that he said that you said that I said," stuff; we are walking side by side in a "community of unity." And it is right here that the issue is exposed. Right here, God's view of His unity and our view of His unity collide. It's in this collision where we must decide what God perceives as a unified brotherhood versus our own perception.

God's version of unity and our perception of unity are not as close as you might think. We perceive unity as all of us joined together, shoulder to shoulder, walking towards the Promised Land of Blessing. Imagine a church side by side frolicking through the fields of Favor, singing, "I'd like to buy the world a coke...." Imagine this church where no one person is bigger or more important than the other. It's the kind of church where everybody's opinion means just as much as everyone else's. There is no such thing as a little "i" or a big "I." In this church, we all are the same and everybody knows our name. This is "unity" at its best, in our perception. This has to be what God is trying to convey to His beloved about living in unity. What a glorious church it is where everyone is just as important as everyone else, right? I don't think this is God's perception of unity that causes "His commanded blessing to flow (Ps. 133:3)." Let me prove it to you.

Imagine a family where the kid's opinion carries just as much weight as the parents. Utter chaos would ensue. Kids are not mature enough to make decisions concerning their own well-being, much less the well-being of the family unit. I was told by a zoo keeper in North Carolina that mother ostriches parent their babies for six months and then leave them to fend for themselves. In other words, everything a six month old baby ostrich has learned is enough to sustain them for life. We, as humans, are not that way. Our children haven't experienced enough life to make educated, rational decisions. It is because of that immaturity, kids cannot be equal in authority to their parents. I am a father of two. I have a little boy, Noah, who is four years old and a little girl, MeKendyn, who is 1 ½ years old. I will never forget the first time I asked my son who was the boss of our house. Noah replied without thinking, "Me. I'm the boss." Immediately, I knew my wife and I had work to do. If you were to ask him today; the conversation, after he joked with you a bit (he's definitely my son) would go something like this:

You: "Noah, who is the boss at your house?"
Noah: "Mommy."
You: "Who is the Big Boss at your house?"
Noah: "Daddy."
You: "Well, who is the Big, Big Boss at your house?"

Noah: He would not respond to you verbally. Noah would take his short little left hand and point to the sky. That is his way of declaring to you, God is the ultimate authority in my home. Even a four year old can grasp there must be a line of authority in order for him to thrive. I work with so many parents that want to be friends with their kids instead of parents. I have never seen that work out well for the kids. But that's another book, someday.

Now, imagine a hospital where the interns or "candy-stripers" have as much right to operate as a seasoned doctor on call. Your baby girl has fallen off of her new red tricycle and sliced her knee wider than a bandage can aid. You look at her tears and her blood and come to the conclusion, a trip to the Emergency Room is absolutely necessary. You rush her to the ER for analysis. A doctor comes in and says, "Susie has a bad cut and needs about 10 staples to stabilize the bleeding." He goes on, "let's get her cleaned up and we'll put them in right now." What peace knowing your baby is in the hands of someone with the authority and the experience to properly treat your precious gift from God. Just as the doctor is about to put in the first staple, a "candy-striper" walks in and tells him to stop. She says, "There is so much blood left in the waiting room that I have decided the leg should be amputated." The doctor couldn't trump her. She is just as important as the doctor. Who is to say his words are more valuable than hers? They are equals. Never mind that she has no formal training. Forget the fact that this candy-striper isn't even qualified to be called a nurse yet. There is no system of authority; therefore there is no one to make the proper, righteous call. Hope becomes the only strategy for sustaining the life and the leg of your baby girl. It is a terrible place to be, when "hope" is your only strategy to be a success.

If no parent would ever allow a child to have the same authority as him/herself, and no doctor, with a half brain, would allow the opinion of a wanna-be nurse to dictate his actions on a patient, then why do we think God has a new system in which His church is to operate. Unity that brings the commanded blessing is when everyone is in their posi-

31

tion under authority. Imagine a human body that has its ears connected to its elbows that are connected to its knee caps. The clinical term for that is "deformity." Deform: to distort the form of; to spoil its natural state. If there has ever been a way to describe The Student Body in this age, it is spoiled from its natural state. God has an alignment that He longs for. He longs for it so much, he says, "life evermore" comes out of His structure of unity. He has set His system in place for us to excel at life. The only "hope" that God relies on, is you and I aligning ourselves, and those we have rule over, in the proper position. Only then do we allow His commanded blessing to flow.

The umbrella of influence

On Father's Day 2006, my pastor read from a poem entitled: "Last Laugh" by Robert Penn Warren. Mr. Warren makes this statement *"When a father's dead, an umbrella's gone."* Mr. Warren is pointing out that every one of us has a covering to give to those that come underneath us. There is an umbrella of influence that you and I have been given by God to walk with for covering those He has entrusted us to help grow. Imagine the largest golf umbrella you can hold. Do you see the alternating black and white stripes? Look at the big logo on the side that says, "This is my influence." Now imagine that all of the people God has entrusted you to train and care for are under that umbrella with you. It is as natural as breathing, the more people that crowd around the center of the umbrella, the lower they must bend down to get underneath for protection. Your umbrella is your influence. People are naturally inclined to get underneath your influence if you are a decent leader. Your influence protects your people from the driving rain and the damaging sun. The question is, "will you open your umbrella and let it become a "first come, first serve" umbrella or will you be strategic and place people in orderly fashion to maximize your umbrella of influence? Will you be the kind of person that understands your arm will get tired, therefore you place Aaron or Her closest to you to help shoulder the weight? Or will you be the kind of influencer that makes sure the strongest stay the driest? Or are you so intimidated by those who are better in areas where you are weaker, you push them out to fend for themselves? Never push those that are strongest away, whether they intimidate you are not. Those individuals would not be in your ministry if they did not see something in you that they need.

Part of the issues I've witnessed over the past decade of mentoring youth pastors are the holes in their umbrella. Just think how useless an umbrella would be if it was full of holes. You may be able to hold it up longer than anyone else in the world, but the fact remains, the elements you are trying to keep from getting onto the ones underneath you are penetrating through the holes in your influence. Just like Joseph, your gifting may put you before the king, but it is your character that will keep you there. Never count on your gift or your charisma to hold something only your character can carry. Look at all the youth pastors today who have fallen by the wayside or compromised their calling because of the holes in their character. One of the most creative youth pastors in my city lost his ministry and split his church, because he had the tools to develop a dynamite program, but did not have the character to stay away from a girl to which he found himself attracted. If there are holes in your character and in your influence, pay the price and do some patch work. You are a youth pastor; I know you're used to hard work.

I believe we all work hard. The challenge of this book is to become the kind of influencer that works smart. Why? Because God is longing to pour on the Student Body so much blessing, favor, and anointing, there will be enough to flow throughout your entire church body.

Blessing, Favor, and Anointing comes from God

You have to understand, God longs to pour over you and your team, blessings like you have never seen before. The psalmist made it very clear that the oil was poured out by God. The oil in the passage represents a blessing that is beyond the normal, human status quo. This oil is also a portrait of the favor of God that He longs for His people to live in every day. This oil is also an image of the anointing God yearns for His followers to use as they operate in their lives, jobs, and callings. I do not believe there is a single person that would pass up the opportunity to have that kind of blessing, that kind of favor, and that kind of anointing saturate their life. Throughout Scripture, you can point to the desire of God for His children to be blessed. He even stated it in Numbers 6:23: "Instruct Aaron and his sons to bless the people of Israel with this special blessing. NLT" In other words, God told Moses, "This is how I want my people to be blessed." His desire is to give you so much favor, so much blessing, and so much anointing that there will not be room enough to contain what He longs to pour out on you and all who follow you. But, you have to be kingdom minded.

He has a Kingdom, not a democracy

One of the hardest things about Christian living in America is determining where democracy is permissible, and where Kingdom living is required. We have an opinion in America about everything. As I write this book, I see the nation of Israel fighting Hezbollah in Lebanon for kidnapping two of their soldiers. They are invading the country of Lebanon with soldiers and bombs. I'm not one to get in debates about political stuff. It's just not my nature. What has me mesmerized by the conflict is the media reporting on how important our nation's opinion is in our own mind. We, in America, are so used to vocalizing our thoughts; I believe we think everyone else actually cares. In our democratic world, everyone has a voice. Everyone has a vote. Everyone has the right to free speech. God's kingdom is just that; a kingdom. If we are not careful, we'll start living out Christianity as a red-blooded American who has the right to do whatever it is we think is right. That is not God's way. Trust me, Christianity is a kingdom and He is king!

Peter on the Day of Pentecost writes in Acts 5:31
31 Him God has exalted to His right hand to be Prince and Savior, to give repentance to Israel and forgiveness of sins.

Paul pens these words in the Book of Colossians 1:16-20
16 For by Him all things were created that are in heaven and that are on earth, visible and invisible, whether thrones or dominions or principalities or powers. All things were created through Him and for Him.
17 And He is before all things, and in Him all things consist.
18 And He is the head of the body, the church, who is the beginning, the firstborn from the dead, that in all things He may have the preeminence.
19 For it pleased the Father that in Him all the fullness should dwell,
20 and by Him to reconcile all things to Himself, by Him, whether things on earth or things in heaven, having made peace through the blood of His cross.

The writer states in Hebrews 1:8
8 But to the Son He says: "Your throne, O God, is forever and ever; a scepter of righteousness is the scepter of Your Kingdom.
10 And: "You, Lord, in the beginning laid the foundation of the earth, and the heavens are the work of Your hands.
11 They will perish, but You remain; and they will all grow old like a garment;

12 Like a cloak You will fold them up, and they will be changed. But You are the same, and Your years will not fail."

The man who perhaps knew him best wrote in John 1:1,3 In the beginning was the Word, and the Word was with God, and the Word was God. All things were made through Him, and without Him nothing was made that was made.

Revelations 5:1-14

6 And I looked, and behold, in the midst of the throne and of the four living creatures, and in the midst of the elders, stood a Lamb as though it had been slain, having seven horns and seven eyes, which the seven Spirits of God are sent out into all the earth.

7 Then He came and took the scroll out of the right hand of Him who sat on the throne.

8 Now when He had taken the scroll, the four living creatures and the twenty-four elders fell down before the Lamb, each having a harp, and golden bowls full of incense, which are the prayers of the saints.

9 And they sang a new song, saying: "You are worthy to take the scroll, and to open its seals; for You were slain, and have redeemed us to God by Your blood out of every tribe and tongue and people and nation,

10 And have made us kings and priests to our God; and we shall reign on the earth."

11 Then I looked, and I heard the voice of many angels around the throne, the living creatures, and the elders; and the number of them was ten thousand times ten thousand, and thousands of thousands,

12 saying with a loud voice: "Worthy is the Lamb who was slain to receive power and riches and wisdom, and strength and honor and glory and blessing!"

13 And every creature which is in heaven and on the earth and under the earth and such as are in the sea, and all

that are in them, I heard saying: "Blessing and honor and glory and power be to Him who sits on the throne, and to the Lamb, forever and ever!"

14 Then the four living creatures said, "Amen!" And the twenty-four elders fell down and worshiped Him who lives forever and ever.

The Revelator writes in Revelations 19:11-16

11 Now I saw heaven opened, and behold, a white horse. And He who sat on him was called Faithful and True, and in righteousness He judges and makes war.

12 His eyes were like a flame of fire, and on His head were many crowns. He had a name written that no one knew except Himself.

13 He was clothed with a robe dipped in blood, and His name is called The Word of God.

14 And the armies in heaven, clothed in fine linen, white and clean, followed Him on white horses.

15 Now out of His mouth goes a sharp sword, that with it He should strike the nations. And He Himself will rule them with a rod of iron. He Himself treads the winepress of the fierceness and wrath of Almighty God.

16 And He has on His robe and on His thigh a name written: **KING OF KINGS AND LORD OF LORDS.**

No matter what you think of this Kingdom and its King, Paul writes in Philippians 2:9-11

9 Therefore God also has highly exalted Him and given Him the name which is above every name,

10 that at the name of Jesus every knee should bow, of those in heaven, and of those on earth, and of those under the earth,

11 and that every tongue should confess that Jesus Christ is Lord, to the glory of God the Father.

Who is this King you ask? Well…
  He is the Boss of bosses.
  He is the CEO of all CEO s.
  He is the Chairman of every Board.
  He is the Chief of chiefs.
  He is the Czar of the czars.
  He is the Emperor of all emperors.
  He is the Mayor of the mayors.
  He is the Monarch of the monarchs.
  He is the Potentate of the potentates.
  He is the Premier in every premier.
  He is the Prime minister of the Prime ministers.
  He is the President of the presidents.
  He is the Ruler of the rulers.
  He is the Sovereign of the sovereigns.
  He is the Sheriff of the sheriffs.
  And He is the Speaker of this House.
  Bottom line: He is King of kings and Lord of lords!
  Terrorists can't kill Him. Why? He's the "bomb!"
  Parliament can't fire Him.
  The House can't impeach Him.
  The Senate can't veto Him.
  NATO can't stop Him.
  His power is absolute.
  His resources are inexhaustible.
  His victory is certain
  His Kingdom is everlasting.
  And I want every politician and atheist to know; He has
  not, is not, and will not be resigning!

That's the King that runs this Kingdom. That's the God
who rules and reigns forevermore. Do you think He really
needs our input? With everything He is, do you think He
really needs America's approval? Don't you know, He is
everything, therefore He knows everything? He's not looking

for anyone to take a vote, much less finding out if He has the popular vote. He's not worried about the majority leaders, He is the majority. He couldn't care less about being politically correct. He's KING and He does what He wills. And His will is what He does. Would you want to align yourself or your ministry underneath anyone or anything else? Can you imagine, if He is all of that, how much blessing, favor, and anointing can flow into the lives of the people who walk in unity and are submissive to the process that puts us into the position to receive this commanded blessing? I think this would be a great time for you to set this book off to the side and just pledge your allegiance to the King. Let Him know you are under His lordship. More than a minister, more than an American, more than a northerner or southerner, more than your social status, more than a color, more than a race, let it be said of you and of me, we will not be defined by what we have or what we wear or what color we are. I will only be defined as His son or His daughter. You know He reigns and He longs for you to position yourself in such a manner that His commanded blessing can flow to you and yours. Oh bless His Holy Name!

— —

I'm Not Fussing!!

➤ Most people regulate "the anointing" for preaching a good sermon or getting emotional in an altar or worship time. The anointing is given for trouble. If you resist this statement, read Isaiah 61 and don't stop after verse 3. The purpose of the anointing is for trouble to be dealt with. You are not anointed to shout, dance, or play Chubby Bunny. You are anointed to stand in extremely difficult troubles and bring freedom, healing, restoration and gladness. Stop being anointed just to "have church."

➢ We Americans have NO clue what Kingdom is really about. I hope that I gave you more than preaching material in some of my statements above! God is not American, nor is He running a democracy. I find it interesting how I have a degree in Christian Education, yet never took one course on Kingdom living. Crazy, I say.

➢ Stop standing at the wrong window waiting to get paid! Ephesians 6:8, "What you make happen for others, God will make happen for you." Stop waiting on your pastor, deacons or council to acknowledge you. Stop trying to let your good deeds and actions be seen by everybody.

What You Need To Do is...

➢ Read as many books on Kingdom Living by Dr. Myles Monroe as you can. It will change your life by renewing your mind

➢ Create your version of, "It's a Flow thing" and begin communicating that down throughout the Student Body. You must begin speaking alignment long before alignment actually happens

➢ Start being a Mystery Miracle worker for your church. Make things happen that need to be done and do your best to not be found out as the one who did it. Whether it is groceries for a needy family or painting the nursery, be a miracle and stop waiting on one.

Chapter 2

You Know, the Problem with Youth Pastors today is…..

"Obey your leaders and submit to them, for they keep watch over your souls as those who will give an account…"
Hebrews 13:17

"Why would I want to be Senior Pastor? I get to have my own church, do my own thing, and be around people I like inside the church, with little to no responsibility for making sure the bills get paid." If I have said that once, it's been hundreds of times over the course of my tenure at this church. Early on in my career as a Youth Pastor, I developed this mentality that I could pastor a youth church, inside the church, without being a part of the entire church. While mentoring dozens of fellow youth pastors, I have witnessed this same mindset as "coffee conversation." I would love to make excuses and say that some misled mentor in my past deluded me into that philosophy. The truth is, I allowed myself to operate in a philosophy that was contrary to God's philosophy. The problem is I was not close enough to the Holy Spirit to hear Him tell me how wrong I was for adopting it into my philosophies of ministry. Instead

of leading teens to a mature walk with Christ, I found myself
continuing in my own adolescence.

All the freedom, none of the responsibility

The greatest way to describe a teenager is an individual
who demands all the freedom they can get, without taking
any of the responsibility that freedom demands. No freedom
comes without cost. It is a truly immature person who
believes there is no price for freedom. "Life, liberty, and the
pursuit of happiness" does not equal my freedom to do, say,
and be want ever it is I want.

Some of my happiest moments are when I am most mis-
chievous. I love to cause trouble. All of my life I have been
labeled as someone to keep two eyes on. As a matter of fact,
the reputation I have with my students goes something like
this: if you flick him, he'll punch you. I am not saying that
is the best way to describe my leadership, however, it is a
pretty accurate description of my revenge. Let me share with
you a testimony to my lack of wisdom in this arena.

It was a typical Saturday night in the middle of the "dog
days" of August, in the buckle of the bible-belt. Just like any
other Saturday, I was spending time with some of the kids
and staff of my youth group. We were hanging out at one of
the youth staff member's home, eating the greasiest pizza
we could find and chasing those slices of "zit-makers" down
with some good ol' sweet tea. It didn't take long before the
girls began trading toenail polish and confidential concerns
(we don't call it "gossip," it's called "sharing.") And we,
strapping, red-blooded, all-American boys, took off to our
vehicle for a few hours of "fun" to do "guy" stuff. Our definition of fun usually is defined by making someone affiliated
with our church scared or uncomfortable. That night would
be no different. There we were, driving in a green Ford
explorer with approximately 11 guys crammed into it. Oh,
and all of us had a paint ball gun sitting in our lap. Yes, I said

all of us! We drove off like a troop of navy seals entering hostile territory. We opened up our weapons, spraying every sign, every building, every oncoming car, and every cow that was close enough to be a target. We launched the phrase, "painting the town" to a whole new level! Flying through Main Street, we stopped just long enough to ensure the safety of our metropolis, by unloading our hoppers on the volunteer Fire Department. When we saw the light in the sleeping quarters come on, we knew our job was a success.

After our training mission was completed, we knew we had to set our sights on someone in our church family that could handle a joke. So with great enthusiasm we targeted one of the biggest pranksters in our church. Let's call him, Andy. Andy was a hard worker with a growing family. Andy had a lovely wife, two sons, and a beautiful baby girl. Yes, Andy worked hard, but he pranked even harder. On that particular Saturday night in August, we decided to bring the game back to him. There it was, 11:45pm and Andy and his lovely family were safely nestled in their beds. Our version of an Army tank slowly rattled through enemy lines onto the sidewalk facing our target's barricade. All sights were locked. All safeties were off. Enemy base was in our cross-hairs. "Charlie" had no clue we were there. All that was needed was, "Fire" to be spoken by the captain, me. "Fire! Fire! Fire!" I yelled. Oh the sound of paint balls splatting in the windows of a worthy foe. Nothing brings me more peace and tranquility than the firing of retaliation. We unloaded all of our ammo and sped off like newly weds to their honeymoon suite. Shouts of victory and hearts bubbling with joy filled the Explorer that night as the tires of our "Mean, Green Stealth Machine" squalled in triumph through the stop light and around the corner.

Our celebration, however, was cut very short. In my excitement and in my ignorance, I forgot that Andy's oldest son, who has autism, has a room in the front of the house we hit. I also, failed to realize that the horror of 9/11/2001 happened just weeks prior. Our entire nation was on edge during that time, and the small town of Fort Mill was no different. Andy's little boy ran out of his room screaming, "They're shooting at us, Mommy!" as he dove into the carpet in the center of the house. With weapon in hand, Andy looked through the window ready to protect his home by any means necessary. As he peered through the window, he saw our escape vehicle, an SUV he was used to being in, speeding off into the night. While we were laughing and rejoicing over our prank, Andy was left to pick up the pieces of the terrified little boy God had given him to protect and He gave me to help disciple.

Hopefully, you have never led an operation as ludicrous as the one I led in 2001. As a matter of fact, I have never heard another youth pastor confess to anything as dumb as what I did. It's my prayer that through my testimony, you will see how thoughtless we can be as student pastors in our position. It's as if, we receive a "get out of jail free" card. We just chalk our dumb decisions up as "being a youth pastor." Meanwhile, someone else has to go clean the messy kitchen, we've left behind.

Needless to say, that Sunday morning in August was consumed with apologies and promises never to allow such immaturity to come to his kids again. This family, my friends, almost left the church because of the actions of this youth pastor. Sure they knew it was all in fun. They were absolutely assured I would never intentionally try to harm their precious little ones. The point was that it *did* happen, and I could have stopped it if I were a responsible, sensible man of God. My stomach aches right now as I scroll through the disappointed glares that were directed towards me in meetings with Andy, his wife, the grandparents, and my boss (pastor). It's no wonder, youth pastors are looked at as a liability in the eyes of their senior pastor.

Why Youth Pastors are a liability to Senior Pastors
Liability is a good word to describe the typical youth pastors in the minds of most senior pastors these days. It's this perception of youth pastors that generates a lot of insecure, self-doubting spiritual leaders for teens. Why is it that we (yes, we) always feel as if we have a target on our back? Why does it feel as if we must tip-toe across a thin sheet of ice every week in the staff meeting? Why is that we were praised when we first got hired about how creative we were, and 8 months later we're looking for moving boxes because we won't conform to the system in place? Why do we have a "walking down the hall, feel something fall" pain hit our stomach every time we receive word that the "Big" guy wants to have a talk? Why does the "music" guy never show up to anything on time, sing the same 4 four songs each month, and never do anything extra in terms of "manual" labor, yet still be the "favorite" in the eyes of the Big Boss? Part of our requirement for good youth pastoring is to think outside the box and try something that's needed, and new. We are an R & D (research and development) department at its best. If I had a dollar put in my budget for every time one of my colleagues and/or pastor has been in my office to mooch off of one of my ideas, I'd have a "well-funded" ministry. Yet, you can't have "trial" without "error". You'll never truly know what works, until you figure out what doesn't. If you and I understand this, why can't the senior guy figure it out?

I do not believe the issue is our creativity. I do not believe the issue is our "thinking outside the box." I do not believe the issue is favoritism to another colleague. I think the issue most senior pastors have with us, is our inability to educate and inform him before proceeding with our agenda. I have been a youth pastor for over a decade at the same church, serving the same pastor. Chunks of my rear-end were taken from me, only after I made a decision or did something that effected my pastor while he was ignorant to what I had going on. It is because of my consistent *blow-ups* that my pastor and staff adopted a new philosophy for our pastoral team: "No landmines."

The longer I'm here in this position, the more other senior pastors ask me for advice on how they should handle their youth pastor. I have even been asked to help give senior pastors ideas on how to push their youth pastor to a place where they want to quit. Consistently, I hear senior pastors ask my senior pastor what is the value of paying youth pastors. In other words, they want to know why they should pay to have more problems. They are asking to see the value of bringing someone on in a full-time or part-time position that, in their eyes, adds no value to the "bottom line" of fulfilling their vision. This question that consistently made its way to my bosses desk eventually ended up being posed to me. And I realized that a classic shrug of the shoulders and an "I don't know" was not sufficient to relieve this nagging question.

On the flipside, youth pastors constantly setup meetings with me to complain about the senior pastor they serve under. I have heard it all. "My pastor doesn't have a vision." "My pastor has too much vision and I can't keep up." My pastor is a micro-manager." My pastor won't tell me anything to do." "My pastor is self-centered." "My pastor is too selfless." "My pastor won't give me any money to operate." "My pastor never tells me no." (I couldn't believe it when he said it as a complaint to me either) The longer I live, the blunter I am becoming. Today, I'll sit down with any youth pastor and listen to what he/she has to say. It is not very long before complaining about their senior pastor ensues. I will allow that individual to whine for exactly 4 ½ minutes. When those 4 ½ minutes are up, I will very rudely interrupt him/her and ask one question. "Did you bring me here to agree with you so you'll feel better, or do you want me to tell you the truth?" Usually, he/she will immediately respond, "I want you to tell me the truth." It's fun to watch the liars squirm when I dive into my opinions on what their problems are. What's funny is the "problem" always turns out to be the same thing when it comes to dealing with senior pastors. It always comes back to who's under authority and who wants to do their own thing. It usually ends with someone getting into alignment or moving on to greener pastures.

Why we move every eighteen months

I was riding back to the office from an appointment today, when I came across Rod Stewart on the radio. In my mind, I knew this was the portion of the book I was going back to write. Ironically enough, I was radio surfing when I heard Rod sing, "You're so far away. Doesn't anybody stay in one place anymore?" It was like I heard teenagers all across America singing this to the youth pastors of today. The average youth pastor is relocating or quitting after only nine months. Why? *Youth pastors are struggling to be under authority.* Few youth pastors today see it as a privilege to be under submission to a man with a vision. American churches, especially, have a hard time learning to operate the way God intended them to. Somewhere along the way, youth pastors developed the mentality, "If things don't work out the way I want, I'll go be a youth pastor somewhere else." As terrible as that mentality is, even worse are the ones I've witnessed staying on and biding their time till they can become a senior pastor themselves and answer to no one. Either way, it's the kids who suffer. As I sit here in the play area of my son's favorite restaurant, and he yells, "Weeee!" coming down the bright yellow twisted slide, I'm trying to imagine how my kids would turn out if they had a new dad rotate in and out of my home every year and a half. Let's face it, the teens we lead are screwed up. The major contributing factor to the demise of these teens is the lack of fathers in the home. Their home life is dysfunctional, and it is that dysfunction that breeds the dysfunctional teens that come through our doors to hear about becoming something different than what they witness each day where they sleep. The problem is these kids are watching pastors, who say they love them and care for them, file in and out just as quickly as the father-figures hooking up with their mommies in their home. So now, we have dysfunctional homes breeding dysfunctional teens. These dysfunctional teens come to church and have dysfunctional youth pastors who are unreliable like every other man in and out of their life. Let me throw something at you the Lord spoke to me early in my ministry when I was offered a promotion to another church. He said, "I put you here to raise my kids as I would, if I was their youth pastor." Now this statement may not be a revelation to you, but to me, it was ministry transforming. In other words, what kind of God do you want me to reflect to these kids? Will I show them that God is here as long as everything is good? Maybe God is the kind of Being who stays around until something or someone better comes along. Or is their God always there, always reliable, and willing to stick with them through it all. I have wanted my teens to see a stable God who is here from start to finish. By the way, the greatest joy of ministry was watching my first graduating class walk in as 6th graders and depart graduating seniors. I don't know how I will act when I get to see them graduate college and move into their adult life. What a joy it will be watching them live and hopefully disciple their own teens, someday.

Don't "dam" it

So what am I trying to tell you? Simply this; take your pastor into consideration before making any decision. Trust me. He would much rather know too much about what you're doing than not enough. And please submit to his authority. Submission is not surrender. It is you understanding that God has a system that He established for you to receive and release His blessing, favor, and anointing. The difference between a small body of believers and a large body is layers of alignment. God's stuff is always compared to a river, not a reservoir. Make it your goal not to stop or dam up the flow of favor into your staff and leaders who are longing to experience that kind of life. Let's start at the top layer and work our way down.

— —

I'm Not Fussing!!

➢ You are way too smart to be making stupid decisions. Faith decisions will always require risk. However, those decisions should only be risky to you and those who want to get out of the boat with you.

➢ If you are in an all-white church in the south, have enough respect to tell your pastor before your only African American student represents Christ dying on the cross in a human video for the Sunday morning services! Yep, I did. Nope, I did not give him advanced notice. Yep, I got whipped in our next staff meeting.

➢ Stop dating different Student Bodies! Get committed and you will be shocked how many stable kids will be the result.

➢ Be intentional. Improvisation must cease to be the standard

What You Need To Do is...

➢ Take all your resumes off job websites

➢ Get liability release forms before anybody jumps on a van in a church sanctioned function

➢ Have a plan at least 2 months before you have to initiate it. Really you should be planning a year out, but I don't want you to be nauseated.

➢ Stop bringing problems to your pastor without recommendations for how to solve them. You will be, or will not be, paid by the problems you solve not bring.

➢ Take ownership of the church campus. You are custodian and a security guard whether you are paid for it or not.

➢ If you are leaving, have a succession strategy for the Student Body. If you do not have a strategy, it's not time to leave.

Chapter 3

Has Anyone Seen My Head?

"Timothy, my son, I give you this instruction...
so that by them you may be strong..."
1 Timothy 1:18

The Psalmist lets us know from the start; the oil of anointing will hit the "head", first. It is this position on the body that receives anything deemed necessary to be released to the body, first. It doesn't splash down on the garments, and then flow up; it hits the "Head," first. It doesn't get poured on the hands to rub on the head; it hits the "Head", first. The body is not held upside down and the oil is poured on the feet; it is poured out by God to the "Head", first. Anything that God wants to release in your live will come to your "head" before it is released to your entire body.

Anything with 2 heads is a monster

"Youth ministry is your very own church without all the responsibility and all the adult children." If I said this once, I've said it a thousand times. In my ignorance, I would boast of all how I had the ability to do my own thing and still have someone else write the checks. What I did not understand was that I was a youth ministry monster.

I had a vision for my volunteer staff that was competing with my pastor's vision. I was trying to pull them one way, while pastor was trying to lead the congregation another. Oh it wasn't a devious plan of attack. I was not out to undermine his authority or vision. As a matter of fact, I would help him fulfill vision as long as it didn't get in my way of accomplishing the goals I set out to achieve. Trust me; I wasn't trying to be divisive. I was just being self-centered.

I was under the assumption I could have a kingdom within a kingdom. I understand more and more why Christ said, "No man can serve two masters. He will love one and despise the other." It wasn't like I was trying to pit my staff against pastor or anyone else. However, when battles came, lines were drawn. When budget money wasn't given in the way my staff and I thought it should, battle lines were drawn. When it came time to "hear the Word of the Lord" on Sunday mornings, I saw my staff "tuning out" the voice of their real shepherd. It's not like my pastor could see the discontent. He was counting on me to make sure this part of the body was fully in line and under authority. What he did not realize was who he put in charge to keep peace was actually the one causing the problem. Let me say again, I was not trying to cause dissension. I had no malice in my heart. I was not intentionally trying to undermine him or his God-given authority. Nevertheless, I *was* causing dissension. I *was* causing strife in the body. I *was* undermining him and his God-given authority. The one he sent to keep peace turned out to be the one causing him problems. I was the ugly second head making us into a monster.

You know, the only place people will go to see a monster is a circus freak show, and I was the ring leader of my very own traveling production. My ministry was a freak show, and "The Body" was the main attraction. The thing about carnivals and side street shows is, you may draw a crowd, but the only types of people who will join and stay connected are freaks themselves! Don't misinterpret me; the rest of the Body seemed to look normal. The rest of the Body tried to function as normal. But no one of real substance would stay and get connected, because they would always have to make excuses for the "monstrous headship" that was attached. Let me help you; YOU ARE NOT THE HEAD! It's not your role to play as a youth pastor, youth leader, youth worker, youth member. Your senior pastor is the head. The movement given from the head is the movement that should take place within the Body.

Your job is not to compensate for the inadequacies YOU THINK your pastor provides in his "headship" position. Your job is not to second guess and undermine what he is trying to do. Your job is to stay in position and make sure everyone under you is falling in alignment. Your job is not to give "lip service" to him in his staff meetings and go do your own thing, your own way, with your own plans being fulfilled by your own team. What you are doing, my friend, is turning your Student Body into a body with two heads. So where do the youth pastors who are facing a shift in the headship position fit? Well...that means you have NO HEAD.

Anything with no head is dead

I was ministering in one of my denomination's youth camp in California a few years back. The Director of the camp had a saying every time we would push the envelope and step over a sacred cow during the service. He would say, "We're dead." When we would make fun of a tradition in the church, he would say, "We're dead." When we would, as the guest ministers, not show up to every single event, he would say, "We're dead." When we would start a huge food fight in the lunch line, he would say, "We're dead." When we snuck out late at night for a cool California swim and get caught, he would say, "We're dead." Friend, when you do not give permission through your submission for your headship to "actively" lead the Student Body, You're dead!

I simply want to make you fully aware of the fact that you MUST have a headship. Youth pastors can't live by teenagers, alone. You require a headship. Every event is DEAD without your Head. Every program is DEAD without your Head. Every discipleship endeavor is DEAD without your Head. Even your effectiveness to move towards *your* next dimension is DEAD without your Head. I am to the place in my understanding of this principle now, that I will not leave my church to go out and minister, teach, or train without my Head blessing that ministry opportunity. There were years when I felt tolerated more than celebrated. There were opportunities that came my way that my own colleagues seemed to not appreciate and want to undermine. But as long as my Head blessed it, I went after it.

This is a HUGE issue for a lot of my peers as they sense their communication skills improving. If I have seen it once, I have seen it dozens of times. The church gets caught in a transition of its headship, and low and behold, the youth pastor jumps up and starts trying to position himself for the headship position. As if "minute to win it" ministry is the qualification that validates your ability to effectively move God's church farther along the path He has laid out for His bride. (yep, that was meant to sting.)

These guys step up and proclaim their "headshipness.", and if the church doesn't follow, they decide they are going 10 miles down the road to start their "own thing." If you fast-forward 5 years into their pastorate, they are still preaching to the same 25 people they left with and are completely miserable. The question that must be answered is "Why?" Because they jumped out of the proper headship and began a work of rebellion that God refuses to bless the same way He would if that "old youth pastor," who wanted to do "his thing," would have been patient and let his head bless his transition. See the problem with doing "your own thing" is that it is only "your thing."

The prodigal son had no idea that he would squander his inheritance. He was convinced he could do better than the father. The prodigal didn't leave his father's covering with all he received thinking that months and years later he would be standing right back in front of that father wanting to be his custodian. The prodigal was out to prove to his father he could handle the responsibility of carrying such an inheritance. The issue was that the prodigal son was ignorant. It is impossible to prepare for something that you have no clue exists. That's why Paul admonishes us to "Not be ignorant concerning…"

There is a saying that came from my personal prayer time recently while I was struggling with the direction my Head was leading our church. I have to admit, it made no sense to me and, to be honest I still, to the day I'm writing this chapter, struggle a little with his direction. So I went above my Head to the Giver of Blessing, Favor, and Anointing and wanted to know for myself if my Head was completely off base with God had actually said to him. I told God how crazy and ridiculous this was and how it would never work. I threatened God with scare-tactics of church members leaving or me quitting over this shift in ministry focus. Like a loving father to his petty, ignorant son, God spoke to my heart this statement: "Son, just because you do not agree, doesn't mean you are right." I responded, "Yes sir. I'm sorry." That chastisement has changed me and my approach to everything that comes from my Head now. I don't want to be surrounded by DEAD objectives. I, like all of you, want to see this Student Body grow and mature. Well it starts by making sure your Head is on right in the Student Body.

Anything with a head that has no activity is a vegetable

I hear it now. "You don't understand. You have a great Head. My Head doesn't do anything and refuses to move into the 20 century. Forget the 21[st,] I just want to get out of the hymnals, convention songbooks, and having to wear a tie during mid-week to preach to teens!" I want to give you three suggestions to consider when you have a head that is in a state of perpetual vegetation.

My first suggestion to those of you who minister to the 21st generation in a 19th century setting (or worse) is simple, do not allow yourself to be victimized by your situation. Anybody can sit around and be paralyzed by what they don't have. You are not a victim in this situation. Where most people see problems, you must start to see opportunities. I LOVE coming into churches that battle the line between traditions and relevance, as an advisor. My time is most effective when the Head asks me to come in to mediate. I'm a relatively young man, but I was raised in the old school church model. I have learned the art of taking a contemporary idea and speaking it in a language that the older generation (Head or church members alike) can understand without being fearful of where it will lead.

"No", most often means, "Not the way you just presented it." You have to learn how to speak King James. Think about it. The word, Ass is in the Bible. I know the context in which it was used. But you can say "Ass" to a group of teens in context of the KJV version and all you will get is snickers and jokes. But you can say, "Ass" to the adult congregation, and not lose your job simply by quoting it in the context of a language they understand and have read themselves. The difference is learning to speak to the audience you are trying to get to listen to you.

My second suggestion is to pray for a resurrection. It is impossible to be mad at someone you pray for all the time. Yep. I just nailed a lot of you again. We are so quick to judge, yet slow to pray. We are so quick to say what's wrong, yet slow to pray. We want to sit around and complain, yet not pray. We want to send inbox prayer requests to our Prayer Warrior Group on Facebook, yet not pray for our Head ourselves. Pray for a resurrection for him. Do not pray for God to remove him or strike him with a disease that puts him in the hospital for months. Pray for a resurrection in his life.

You have no idea what he is facing. You have no idea what he has been going through. You have no idea what his marriage is like and what battles of the mind he is trying to overcome. Pray for him. Bless him. Check in on him. He's the Head you have.

#3 Take care of your Head; it's the only one you've got

My Head's favorite soft drink is Diet Dr. Pepper. He is a coffee coinsure. His favorite coffee shop is Dunkin Donuts, but he will drink Starbucks regular coffee with cream. There is a specific amount of cream he likes, so the best thing is to bring him a separate cup of just cream for him to pour in himself. His dry cleaner of choice is Georgetown Cleaners in Love's Plaza. To him, they do the best job. Men's Wearhouse is where he buys his suits. He shops online for his mono-grammed white dress shirts. Hampton Inn is his choice of hotels to stay in. He is a rewards guy for points. Reading fantasy books is his hobby of choice, unless you want to buy him stocks to trade. The best present I ever bought him was a year of free carwashes at a local Autobell. I have hand-washed his car. I have taken his car to have an oil change before he left on a trip. I have filled his tank full of gas at my expense. I have left my stuff in my car, so I could help him carry his one briefcase in. I hold his door every chance I get. I will eagerly be his driver to meetings or conventions. I have left appointments waiting on me to return so I could run boxes to his car for him. I have fed his dog and cat while he was out of town on vacation. I have left service to go buy him a bottle of water while he was preaching in the pulpit because he seemed to be on the verge of becoming parched. His favorite Sunday lunch is a drive-thru at a local fast food chain. He ends each of his weekends by eating from the varieties of individual tubs of ice cream. I bought him his iPad. Every new App I purchase that is relevant to the craft of preaching, I let him know about or try and gift it to him through iTunes. Why is this important for you to know? Am I bragging about how great I am at being under my Head? Am I a "monkey-boy?" Am I trying show you how much of a sycophant I am? Am I trying to tell you to be a slave? ABSOLUTELY NOT!! I am merely trying to get you to see ways where you can take care of your Head of the Student Body. He or she is the only Head you have, and it is very important for you to take care of your Head.

I was in a leadership class held by Pastor Clint Brown. He made a statement that shaped my perception of Blessing your Head. He said, "If you ever want someone to carry your bags, you better be carrying someone else's bags now." That statement is the crux of this entire chapter. Learn to carry the bags of your Senior Pastor and watch how many people line up to carry yours, as you carry his.

In light of all this, I would like for you to write a letter of resignation to your Senior Pastor as Head of the Student Body. Let your Senior Pastor know that from this point on, you will not being doing your "own thing." Your cues and your plays will be made from his/her playbook. Let your Senior Pastor know that you are on a quest to get the Student Body of your church aligned properly for the Commanded Blessing of Psalm 133 to be unleashed over the Student Body. And the first step is for you to know your role and operate solely in that position. If you have second guessed him/her, spoke against his/her vision, or resisted his/her authority over the Student Body, repent before him/her and tell your Senior Pastor how God made a statement through a "King James Donkey" that has revolutionized your per-spective on the Student Body. That statement being, "Just because I do not agree, doesn't mean I'm right." Step back and watch "the oil" begin to flow down to you.

— —

I'm Not Fussing!!

➤ How presumptuous can you be to sit and critique the preaching of God's word through God's man? You have been preaching 3 years. This man/woman has been doing it for decades and you think you can do it better? Please.

➤ You sit around complaining about raising funds for 8-15% of what your Head has to raise in a year. Don't open your mouth in complaints about budgets. You sound stupid.

➤ Stop making the Student Body a FREAK SHOW. You are not the Head.

What You Need To Do is…

➤ Write a resignation letter to your Head of leading the Student Body. Let him/her know you will be intentionally taking signals from their leadership from now on. There is a no compete clause from here on out. Apologize for your ignorance while you are at it.

➤ Find out your Head's favorite something and keep him or her stocked.

➤ At least once a week, pop in his/her office and see if there is anything you can do to lighten their load that week.

➤ Shoot a text (if he/she isn't 80 years old & still has a rotary phone at their home) letting him/her know you have been in prayer for his/her family once a month.

➤ Get his/her keys every 6 months and have his/her car washed and filled up with gas

➤ Give him/her a coupon book filled with redeemable benefits from students and staff in your Student Body every year for Pastor Appreciation Day.

Chapter 4

Know Your Role

"You speak to us, and we will listen..."
Exodus 20:19b

Not Head, but really close

The beard is representative of the mouthpiece that God uses. The mouthpiece is a part of the Headship and has a direct attachment to what sends instruction to the Student Body. You are the mouthpiece of the Student Body. A vision can't stay inside the Head, yet the Head has an expectation that the vision will be captured by the heart of the people. It MUST be articulated by the mouthpiece. It is so important to have words go forth; God, Himself, spoke creation into existence. In other words, God had a thought, but what made that thought a reality was the "Let there Be" that took place. You are not the Head, but your role is still vital to the overall success of the Student Body's alignment. Let me give you a few Biblical examples of what I'm saying.

Mouthpieces in the Bible

The fire that fell from Heaven for Elijah versus the prophets of Baal was not because of the altar. The fire fell as a result of the words prayed from the mouthpiece.

It was Caleb and Joshua's report of the Promised land that captured the heart of the people to pursue the Land flowing with milk and honey. However the other 10 spies that came with the negative report of the land eliminated the pursuit and thus compromised them achieving the promise for decades.

Adam was talked into the sinful act of eating the fruit, not by the snake but by the one who had his heart.

It was the kiss of Judas that sealed the betrayal of Christ.

It was the words from Peter on the Day of Pentecost that launched the Church.

Esther's words of respect positioned her for a private audience with the King.

Ruth's verbal refusal to leave Naomi is what brought her to the field of Boaz.

David's songs.

Solomon's articulated judgments before the people.

Jeremiah's boldness to speak.

John the Baptist's riverside sermons.

Every single Sunday all over the world, ministers of this Gospel use the "foolishness" of preaching to peel back the blindfolds of sinners and expose the Light and Love of this Glorious Christ, proving how important it is for there to be a mouthpiece to the Headship of the Student Body. And you, youth pastor who is full-time or not, are that mouthpiece who must speak.

You're the mouthpiece - Speak up

Since it is your role, speak up. You are THE distinguishing factor for your Student Body and every other student ministry in your area. What makes your Student Body unique is YOU! You have an opinion and you have a delivery, so deliver your opinion. I'm growing weary of every Student Ministry looking and acting the same. You are a distinct creation of God, so your ministry should have a feature that is your imprint. That imprint is made by what you speak.

There is a fast food joint here in my area called Jack in the Box. Jack in the Box is crazy. You can go there at any moment and order anything from egg rolls to breakfast to cheeseburgers to Mexican food. Bottom line, if you want it you can get it at Jack in the Box. It's got everything you are looking for. They pride themselves on being so diverse that no matter what your family is in the mood to eat, Jack in the Box can make everyone happy. Great concept. My issue with Jack in the Box is everything is fried in the same grease, grilled on the same stove, packaged the same way, and sitting under the same heat lamps. After a while, the egg rolls taste like the French fries and the French fries taste like the onion rings. Although the variety is great in theory, the deliveries of authentic tastes are very disappointing.

In contrast, I just had lunch a few moments ago at a restaurant called, Just Chicken. You can imagine. This fast-food joint only sells chicken. Fried chicken, grilled chicken, chicken tenders, chicken legs, chicken wings or an egg (baby chicken in case you forgot) and cheese biscuit is all that this place sells. It truly lives up to its name, JUST CHICKEN. What this company is saying is, "Hey we make chicken. If you want chicken, it's what we are staking our entire company on, because we're good at it. If you don't want chicken, this isn't the place for you."

I believe most Student Body Mouthpieces are Jack in the Box employees when they should be Just Chicken. You are so busy trying to be everything to everyone that you are diluting your flavor. The flavor of Student Ministry has become so thinned there is little difference in the sound of the Catholic youth guy versus the Baptist youth pastor versus the Pentecostal youth pastor versus the charismatic youth pastor versus the Methodist youth pastor. When the truth is you should be JUST CHICKEN. Some people may leave. Some may not want chicken. Some people may not ever come through your doors again. But there are people who are dying for the words you distinctively give. Your "Let There Be" is precisely what they are looking for.

Over and over again I hear a similar statement in regard to the Shabbach Youth conferences. Colleagues and peers of mine often say, "There is nothing out there like what you are doing." In other words, I am distinctive. Why would I want to do a conference like Acquire the Fire or any other huge youth conference or fest? I can't compete with them. The awesome thing is I don't have to compete. I have the niche in the market for what I provide and I'm the best me there is every going to be. Nobody and I mean nobody can beat me at being me. I am the best Glenn Walters there has ever been or ever will be. Like Popeye, "I am who I am." You also have a voice that is distinctive. Use it. Use it wisely, but use it.

A place for nutrition and health to enter the body

The mouth is where nutrition and health enter the Student Body, so you must be careful what you allow to be taken in to be digested. This is a big deal because what you allow in will affect much more than just you. I believe the role of the Mouthpiece is as vital to the overall success of the Student Body as the Head is.

The Head sends signals throughout the entire Student Body with instructions on how to function. It is the Mouthpiece that provides the substance necessary to the Student Body to operate in that function. I have gone on hospital calls where someone with a fully functioning brain did not have the energy throughout the rest of their body to move because they were starving their self to death. I have witnessed cancer patients who had fully functioning brains not have enough stamina to get out of bed because of the lack of oxygen being taken in their mouth. Even in my own family, I have witnessed a loved one so overwhelmed by the struggles beyond her control that she stopped eating and became more and more malnourished until she was skin and bones.

Take fasting as another example of the importance of the mouthpiece. Every other part of your body, including your head at times, is telling you to eat and give nourishment to the body. It is the resistance of your head and the refusal of your mouth working in sync that puts the whole body in alignment. You, functioning in your role, can bring life or death.

Life or death – your role decides

Proverbs 18:21 tells us, "Life and death are in the power of the tongue." You decide. You determine whether the Student Body is being fed or destroyed. It is the role and function of the Mouthpiece that determines who lives or dies, not the Head. You provide the substance for the Student Body to operate under the Head's authority. Your role is too critical for you to be playing "head games." You have life to give. There is an entire Student Body who needs you to be the part of the Student Body that only you can be. Your kids are not looking for another voice. They are not sitting in a conference or fest wishing you sounded like someone else. Only you can be you, and no one can beat you being you, so long as you are honestly being yourself. Your job is too crucial for you to be insecure. Unless God called the Student Body to a fast, they can't afford for you to starve them because you are not fulfilling your role. Your Head can't be the mouthpiece of the Student Body. He/she has to get signals everywhere. He/she needs you to be the "life giver" of substance to sustain the signals.

The key word of Proverbs 18:21, in my opinion, is "power." We have a young boy in our church that has been deaf from birth. Through a miraculous surgery and lots of patience by his parents and grandparents, he is now learning how to hear and communicate verbally with other people. Jesse is a cool little kid. His mom and dad adopted him as a baby. They didn't know something was wrong with his hearing until they realized he had no power to speak properly. He wasn't speaking because he wasn't hearing. This great little kid would walk around angry and frustrated at church. His grandmother, the office manager at our church, would bring him in from time to time and he would just yell or point in hopes someone would get the clue as to what he was asking for. I watched this family live very taxed by the hardship of the absence of little Jesse's power to speak. One day, after the Lord spoke to me in my prayer time about Jesse and his family, I called his dad and left him a message on his mobile. I simply told Jesse's dad, "I was praying for you guys this morning and the Lord spoke to me to tell you He is in this."

Fast forward a couple years to this past Wednesday night. As I am walking across campus to go into the Family Life Center for our pre-service staff meeting, Jesse's dad stops me by his car. I had the privilege of spending a couple moments talking to him and Jesse. After a little small talk, Jesse's dad's tone change and tears began to fill his eyes. He said, "Do you remember the day you called me and told me God was in this whole situation we were facing with Jesse?" I replied, "Of course." He said, "The Lord reminded me of that this morning in my prayer time. While at my job a lady came to me asking for prayer over a very difficult situation with her daughter. God brought your words back to me again, as if I should repeat them to her, so I did. Pastor Glenn, when I spoke the words, "God is in this" to her she began to weep. It reminded me of my tears when I got your voicemail and you shared those same words with me." He said, "I want you to know that you were right and God has shown His power in this, and He continues His faithfulness in the lives of a family you don't even know." After he and

I embraced I reached over and slapped high-fives with Jesse as he told me "Goodbye."

Change took place for Jesse's family as he gained the power to communicate to his family. Jesse's dad was renewed when I operated in the power of the Mouthpiece in regard his home. Jesse's dad brought life into the home of a lady struggling with her situations by operating in the power of being a mouthpiece to her in a time of need. Your role is too important for you to be anything other than who you are and what He positioned you to be in the Student Body.

— —

I'm Not Fussing!!

- ➤ Words are thoughts revealed. Your job is to articulate the concepts in the Head. The Head is to make concrete the precepts given by God. Too deep? Process it.
- ➤ Words take on flesh. A child will live up to, or down to, what is being spoken into them.
- ➤ Make sure your words are creating what you want produced. If not, change your language.

What You Need To Do is...

- ➤ Ask some of your close staff members if they pick up on any contradictions in what you say and where your Head is going.
- ➤ Ask your Head if he/she has EVER had someone from the Student Body come to them with a concern about you promoting disunity to your Headship.
- ➤ Read the book, "Does Your Tongue Need Healing" by Derek Prince
- ➤ Kill sarcasm in your services. Let your words give healing. This isn't easy. I still fight this.
- ➤ <u>Demand</u> your Head speak to the Student Body at least one time a year.

Chapter 5

Turning Heads

*"after 6 days Jesus took with Him Peter,
James and John and led them up..."*
Matthew 17:1

I love the term given for commentators on news channels these days. They call them "Talking Heads." The implication of that term is hilarious to me. What people are saying is, "These people sit around and talk, but do not have any power to act." I love it because the people who came up with this term see those people for who they really are. These Talking Heads sit in front of a camera for hours and whine, complain, argue, take shots at other people, all kinds of other really dramatic stuff. But at the end of the day, all they have is an opinion with no power to change anything. Oh I watch as well as you. Some are very witty and sarcastic. Others are just plain stupid. It is incredibly entertaining. But at the end of the day, those talking heads are impotent ideologists. They fuss and get mad and threaten, but really they are just the Wizard of Oz with a lot of smoke, fireworks, and noise, having no power to move beyond being just a "Talking Head."

Unfortunately, the youth pastors that I have the opportunity to go and train from time to time are the exact same way. They are just "Talking Heads." They have great minds and witty sermons, but there is no Student Body that is in motion. Oh there's the smoke and fireworks, and whining and taking shots at other Student Bodies, but there is no power to act. So it begs to ask the question. "Why?"

Truth be told, it is because the Mouthpiece is doing everything. You are limiting your Student Body's ability to move because you are a severed Head. You can think and you can talk, but you can't move! In other words you need a staff that you trust enough to take some of the leadership roles. The major difference between small churches and larger churches is not money, its layers of authority. Why does everyone have to answer to you? Why are you so important that you have to be the focus of every event, decision, rehearsal, meeting, and worship service? I hear you, "Because I'm the only one who can do it." Hear me, "NO YOU ARE NOT!!" You are ridiculous and need to grow up.

I went to our local Post Office recently in a borrowed vehicle. I noticed one of my beautiful teenage girls sitting in her mom's van in the parking lot. She had no clue I was in her world at that moment. It's funny what people do when they don't know someone is watching. As I was gathering my things to take in to the post office, I was trying to devise my plan of how I was going to scare the "boo-boo" out of her. It's kind of my calling card with my kids. I love to prank and scare people. It's one of the perks of being in youth ministry, in my humble opinion.

As I finished gathering my items to mail and the plan had been set, I looked over at her one more time to make sure she hadn't noticed me. She definitely didn't notice I was there! She had her BIG TOE in her mouth biting her toenail! She was filing her TOENAILS down by peeling them with her MOUTH! If you do not know me, I HATE FEET!!! I don't like to look at them. I definitely don't want to smell them. And I surely do not want them in my (or anyone I talk to's) mouth. I was grossed out to the point I didn't even speak to her. I skipped my plan, just ran in and did my thing. To this day, I have not spoken to her about it.

That story, however, is indicative of a typical Student Bodies today. The Mouthpiece is so important that we have to be the vessel used for trimming toenails! Friends, we have to learn how to empower the staff. If you and I are going to have a Student Body and not just a Talking Head, we must learn to prioritize the staff we are empowering to operate as the Neck our body needs.

The Neck has two specific roles to play in the Student Body. First it is the portal for the Headship to the rest of the Student Body. Secondly, the Neck is the pivot by which the Head changes focus.

The Portal

The Neck is the top layer needed in the Student Body between the Headship and the rest of the Body. The Headship rests on the key personnel that make up the neck. The Neck is the conduit for three key components to the rest of the Student Body. It is the passage way for nutrients, it centralizes the intelligences for distribution, and it is where body muscle begins. All of these components are mission critical to how the Student Body receives and responds. Without a Neck operating effectively, communication between the Head and the rest of the Student Body is not even possible. If one vertebra is fractured or out of place, it throws off the balance and comfort of the entire body. The Neck is crucial in its role as the portal.

The Pivot

The Neck is also responsible for pivoting the Headship. Think about it. You Head does not move. Your vision does not change. Your perspective does not change unless your Neck begins to pivot. These "inner 3" leaders MUST have the respect and the ears of the Headship in order to help shift direction. But in order for a real shift to happen, you must know who your inner 3 are and how the rest of your Student Body aligns themselves under them. In other words, you must begin to prioritize your staff.

Prioritizing your staff

Your Student Body should flow like a network marketing strategy. It should be small up top and become bigger as it flows downward. When I began this journey in developing my Student Body, it came from the long hours of trying to meet with large groups of teens and every one of my paid and volunteer staff members one on one. I had to learn the hard way, the transition of information and direction is not from me to 30 paid and volunteer staff members all in one step. I had to develop an Inner 3 Leadership to count on. This principle came right from the Jesus approach to His disciples.

Inner 3's to Jesus

Matthew 17 gives the account of Jesus taking Peter, James and John up on the Mount to pray. Jesus could have very easily brought everyone up there with him. All the disciples could have accompanied him. The very crowd He just admonished to "deny, take up your cross, and follow Me" could have, in fact, "followed Jesus" up the Mount to pray. I mean if there was ever anything a great crowd should witness, it should be the prayer and "Transfiguration" of Jesus. That way a mighty revolution could have taken place and there could have been even more witnesses of His power. But He didn't. He chose an "inner 3." I love this illustration of great "inner 3" modeling by Jesus. Watch the steps Jesus took them through to show them how special they were.

1. He enticed them with prayer – Jesus wanted them to know up front, He was taking them on a spiritual journey where time with Father God is a must.
2. He separated them from the pack - He asked them to come on a journey that not everyone was invited on. Thus, letting them know you are different than even the other disciples.
3. He took them up a mountain – The path to seeing something special that no one else will get to see will require an elevation of their lives first.
4. They saw Jesus in a way no one else got to see Him – He revealed Himself in an intimate way so they could see His Divinity. Our roles are reversed. Most people see us in our Priestly garments, but the inner 3 need to see you in your "humanity."
5. He allowed God to deal with Peter's hasty decision making – Jesus gave them permission to suggest and dream.
6. The inner 3 heard from God for themselves and were scared – Jesus positioned His inner 3 to get their own "God Word" and get freaked out.
7. When Jesus saw them freak, He touched them – There was an intimate connection between Jesus and His inner 3 to the point that He could read their emotions and wanted to encourage them.
8. They looked but only saw Jesus – This is another example of alignment. It wasn't necessary for them see Father God. Jesus carried the "signals" His Head was sending.
9. Jesus told them not to talk about it, yet – Jesus gave them the inside scoop long before it was public knowledge.
10. They kept asking questions after the experience and He kept answering – Jesus shows us that not only do the inner 3 need to be in for the long haul, but He had

to get them completely at peace with Him and their alignment to Him.

Who are the 3 who have the vision of who you are?

Peter, the muscle, James, the intelligence, and John the nurturer became the Neck (inner 3) to the body that Jesus put together. So who are yours? My current model is broken down between my Middle School, High School and College Pastor. Since I am currently the High School Pastor and Mouthpiece for the Student Body as a whole, my personal assistant is the third person of my inner 3.

I hear people say often, "I can't let people in." You have to allow your inner 3 in. The only way they will ever be conduits for you is if they can understand what you are trying to change. The only way you will give them permission to pivot your focus is if they are allowed into your personal world. The only way that this can happen is if they get a vision, not for what you want to do, but for who you are, personally.

Show them your undershirt, not your underwear.

I have people always try and figure out how far is too far and how open is too open. My friend, Israel, summed it up best in my opinion. "Show them your undershirt, just not your underwear." Sitting here at the beach trying to finish this book, I have taken multiple breaks to drive along the ocean in a golf cart and walk along the coastline to clear my head. Because I am at Myrtle Beach, SC the amount of "wife beater" t-shirts on the beach is endless. For those of you not from "Redneckville," wife-beater shirts are those undershirts that are sleeveless and resemble a tank top. They are called, "wife beaters" because most often when you watch the TV show, "Cops" there is always some drunk getting arrested for a domestic assault usually in one of those undershirts. The point is, it's personal to show off your undershirt, but it's not so personal that everyone is shrieking at you in your "unmentionables." There are some things you will NEVER be able to share. There are some personal struggles that you CAN'T divulge. There some frustrations with your Head that you MUST NOT reveal. Yet you still must let your inner 3 into your personal world, just maybe not your private one. As you find that balance, you must delegate leadership to your inner 3, not duties.

Delegating Leadership, Not Duties

Let's face it. Being THE MAN is not as fun as it sounds. Like Clark Kent, I would rip my dress shirt, show my BIG "S" and fly to "every kitty stuck in a tree or damsel in distress" singing, "here I come to save the day!" The issue is when you are the answer man, EVERYBODY COMES RUNNING TO YOU WITH ALL OF THEIR QUESTIONS!!!

I have found a secret in a "delegating" style of leadership that no professor or mentor in my life has shared with me to this point. I merely stumbled upon it, but have found it to be incredibly effective at developing leadership beneath me. Now I have to warn you up front, this secret REQUIRES balance in your own life. You can "overuse" this method and become a self-serving jerk that soon finds his leadership obsolete because no one thinks you care. If you are a good leader you are constantly looking for the opportunities to release to your inner 3 to take initiative and make decisions. We can fix wrong decisions. What irks me in inner 3 leadership is when he/she makes NO DECISION! Why would ANY leader call, designate, or need an inner 3 leader if he/she doesn't have the fortitude to make a decision inside their delegated leadership role. This secret will be a paradigm shift for a lot of you who love the "superhero" status because it will force you back into plain clothes more than tights and capes. It will also be a shift for my guys (and gals) who live to make sure EVERY "i" is dotted and EVERY "t" is crossed. Why? There is a powerful transformation that takes place when you let those you lead freak-out, instigate a decision, or even fail by lying crippled like the lame man at the pool, unable to make a decision, thus compromising the issue all together.

Okay, okay. Enough introducing the concept, let me give it to you.

I have found that most leaders under someone else's leadership go through 3 phases in dealing with an issue/decision/conflict directly in front of them.

Phase 1 - FREAKOUT! - Most inner 3 leaders are so drawn "to the butt" at the beginning of their new role, nothing you do will seem to have any flaws or discrepancies. In their eyes, everything you do is "magically delicious!" (- Lucky Charms, I love them!!)So they do not take the time to watch and learn how you navigate through unforeseen issues. They have not taken the time to watch you pause and put this issue through all of your integrity filters before you react. Just by the sheer fact you placed them in charge, FREAKOUT is a part, every time. By the way, FREAKOUT is a good thing because it shows you they genuinely care about the success of what they are leading. If they are apathetic, then you have bigger issues. This FREAKOUT sends them immediately to Phase 2.

Phase 2 - Call Me(you) - If you pick up the 1st time they call , you are in charge! If you are in charge, then why do you need to develop the person who is calling. All they are is a "worker bee" for you. You, my friend, delegate duties, not leadership. Duties fall more in the role of the Shoulders of the Student Body and we will address that in the next chapter. When you have delegated leadership to your inner 3, it is their time to lead. They will not do it the way you would do it. They will not lead just like you. Hopefully you have instilled the same integrity filters in them after a while, but they will not be little clones of you, so relax. When they are in the heat of battle, don't pick up their phone call. Check the voicemail and figure out if it is an emergency or an emotional reaction to you not being there as their superhero. If it's a kid threatening to jump off the top of the church, return the call. If not, do yourself and your inner 3 a favor and stay out of the heat. Otherwise, you are the mom with the 9 year old child who is still breastfeeding! It's weird and nobody wants to be around that! If you will hang on, your silence will take them to Phase 3.

Phase 3 - They work to resolve the issue or make the decision. - THIS IS WHAT YOU WANT IF YOU ARE DELEGATING LEADERSHIP TO YOUR INNER 3, and not just a delegator of duties!! Then they will come back to you for approval or a beating for the decision they made. Be careful if they made the wrong decision. How you handle this moment will determine if they will ever do it again. This is your moment to teach them YOUR filters for good decision-making. Also, you MUST cover for their bad decision!! A good coach gives his kids ALL the credit when they win, and he takes ALL the heat when they lose! In contrast, if they make the RIGHT decision, celebrate them and let them have all the credit. The better they look, the better your leadership looks and the better the Student Body is getting at not needing the Headship to be there for everything!

Now let me finish this "don't abuse this leadership secret" thing. When it comes to leadership, don't answer in the heat. If they are going through something personally, or they are operating in delegated duties, that's when you have to be close by. Be sure after the delegated leadership issue is completely over, you communicate to him/her why you did not answer when they called. Don't make excuses or lie, just simply let them know you TRUSTED him/her to make a call, even if it was the wrong one. Trust me. After years of developing my inner 3 leaders though delegated leadership, they will thank you later!

Although you have to delegate leadership into your inner 3, you must also begin to align the rest of your staff to take on the task of "Shouldering" the delegated duties of the Student Body.

— —

I'm Not Fussing!!

➢ Have enough security in who you are to let others get some credit. The greatest example of your caliber of leadership is when you are nowhere to be seen, especially when accolades are being given from your Head.

➢ Stop being the Google of the Student Body. You shouldn't be the search engine for all of the questions. Find opportunities to send staff and students towards your inner 3.

➢ Your role is not to be buddies with these guys. The moment you cross that line, you have lost your influence to lead through tough times. Trust me, I've made this mistake.

What You Need To Do is...

➢ Have a Student Emphasis Sunday in the main service and have NO part of the platform duties. Empower your staff and students to be in the spotlight (with excellence) and you sit beside your Head on the front row and watch with him/her. Let all the leading be done by your inner 3

➢ Have a consistent meeting with the inner 3, so they can emerge as 1 unit, not 3 interest groups.

➤ Always give them the scoop on what's coming in advance.

➤ Put together at least 2 events per year that will force your inner 3 to work together and be the leaders in charge.

➤ Start giving your inner 3 opportunities to lead segments of your staff meeting.

Chapter 6

Shouldering the Mission

"It would not be right for us to neglect the ministry of God in order to wait on tables. Brothers, choose ... we will turn this responsibility over to them."
Acts 6:2-3

O ne of the things I get most complimented for in the Student Body of my church is how many volunteer staff members I have "Shouldering" the load. Our ratio is almost 1 staff member for every 12 students who are a part of the Student Body. A Student pastor at his best may be able to effectively disciple 70 students by his/herself. Who wants to just have 70 students? If you are ever going to grow to the full potential of God's view of your Student Body, delegating duties will be a must. It is imperative that you allow leaders to lead and lifters to lift. Understand this; you do not need a staff full of leaders. You need leaders but not a staff full of them. A staff filled with just leaders will be incredibly difficult to manage. Leaders have their own ideas and their own way of doing things. That's cool, except when you need the weight of the ministry to just get "Shouldered."

Where the work gets done

Your youth workers are simply that, workers. They are there to fulfill a specific task for the betterment of the Student

Body. If it's preparing food for an event or picking up kids in your newly launched bus ministry, the work must get done. The disciples were sitting around in Acts 6 realizing they were not being effective in their calling because they were too busy doing work that someone else could do. They understood every time they left their prayer and study of the Word for the sake of busing tables, it was a disservice to this Gospel. Serving tables is important. Without the table being set and the food being prepared no one can come and eat on time. I'm with you on the importance of table service. Go to your favorite restaurant and let the table service be poor and you will walk away wondering if you should ever go back. **It is a sign of a poor establishment when the owner is out busing tables.**

The owner should not be arrogant to think he should not humble himself to a "bus boy" status. But it should be a huge red flag in his leadership when the person who has to have a "big picture" vision is focused on a task anyone with a strong back can accomplish. And in contrast, you don't want the waitress carrying the pressure of serving her tables, taking care of her guests and washing the dishes out in back. I am trying to get you to understand that there should be a standard purpose all of your staff are running towards, but that does not mean they all have the same gifting, impact and influence over the Student Body.

All men are created equal, but all staff are not

Instinctively, we want everyone to have a voice and everyone to have equal say in matters of concern. But you and I both know that is not the case. How you ask? When is the last time you have been invited into a council or deacon's meeting to help set your church's annual budget projections? It's not that you are not important. It's that your opinion in this particular matter doesn't really count. The same should be true in your development of your volunteer staff God has sent you to Shoulder the workload of this Student Body.

If you are going to stay in alignment and have the flow of this blessing, favor, and anointing not get dammed, you MUST determine your levels of staff and the requirements for each level. One of the vital reasons I have such a large volunteer base is because everyone doesn't have to show up to everything all of the time. I don't want my snack lady in a creative strategy session. Likewise, I do not want my creative guy making snacks. Why would I want my sound man in my student leadership group? Why would I want my 8th grade Christian Education teacher up in the sound booth for our mid-week production meeting? You have to use sense when you are working through your levels of leadership. Below is how I have broken down the Shoulders of our Student Body.

Level 1 staff
  -They are an inner 3 of one of my inner 3.
  -They have a staff to Shoulder their workload
  -They have a strong core of students who look to them
  for guidance.

  Examples: Drama Director over our 5 drama teams/ Production director over all 3 weekly Student Ministry Services /Christian Education Leader over all 8 grade level classes and the three teachers per class

Level 2 staff
  -They fulfill a specific role on a weekly or monthly basis
  for one of my inner 3.
  -They Shoulder one or more delegated duties for one of
  my inner 3.
  -They have articulated a specific calling for a specific
  dimension of the Student Body
  -They have students who look to them for accountability

Examples: Hip-hop drama leader / grade level C.E. teachers / Praise and Worship leader for Middle school praise team / Snack lady / Family Life Center Setup captain / Small Group leaders

Level 3 staff
-They Shoulder one task quarterly or annually for the Student Body.
-They are a chaperone or a resource for a specific event.
-Students only go to them during that annual or quarterly duty is being fulfilled.

Examples: Weekend Retreat chaperones / host house for an event / cooks for an event / boat owner who meets us at lake for our High School Senior Lake Day

Notice the diversity in duties being delegated. I don't need everyone doing everything. If they will stay in their position and Shoulder the load they committed to, no one else will be burned out by having to be here with students for every single thing we do. I'm not looking to play Checkers, I want to be a Chess champion.

Checkers versus Chess
Chess, by far, is a more sophisticated game than Checkers. In Checkers, every piece is exactly the same. Each piece is the exact same color. Each piece has the exact same design on the top and bottom. Each piece can only move forward to the right or to the left. At each move, each piece determines whether it should stay, move forward, jump an adversary or be expendable so the entire game can be one or another piece can be crowned a king.

In contrast, Chess has completely unique pieces. There are a few that are identical, but for their particular function, it is imperative that they be duplicates. The pieces move in different manners. Some move at angles. Others have the ability to move straight ahead all the way across the board if need be. While still, others can only move one space in one direction. It takes a strategy to play Chess.

My 9 year old son can get the concept of Checkers. In comparison, I still struggle with the function of each piece in Chess, much less trying to explain it to my son. I think this is an issue for most Student Bodies I have encountered over the years. They would prefer to play with immature kids, then have a strategy (that will take time to teach) so the Student Body can be as sophisticated as possible. Pay the price to set the trajectory for where God is pouring His oil out, and build an effective strategy for all the key players and staff to be able to function on the Chess board.

It really is easier than you think. The only person who needs to know how all the pieces move is you. The knight is responsible for knowing his own rules of engagement. The rook, the queen, the king, and even the lowly pawns only have to know what moves they are to make. You control the board, let them only have to worry about what they are directly trying to achieve.

Massage Them Shoulders!

I want to give you a few tips on ways to keep those volunteers inspired to keep carry the weight of the Student Body forward. Let's keep it real. These men and women are the make or break for you, personally. How much work you do is based upon how much load these wonderful people carry. How much time you have to spend in prayer and study of the Word is all contingent upon the amount of work the Student Body Shoulders can handle for you. These guys are crucial for you. In no way am I trying to down play how vitally important each role of the Student Body is. We are just different components of this same body. The moment you begin taking the Shoulders for granted is the moment you will see more work coming your way. Let me end this chapter with a few suggestions on how to "massage the Shoulders" of the Student Body.

First of all, you must give the Shoulders your time. If your staff is going to ever carry your heart, they must first have your time. Set a schedule on your personal calendar to make a monthly personal contact to each of your Shoulder staff. It can be as simple as creating a closed Facebook group of your staff where only they will receive words of encouragement and prayers from you.

Secondly, do not over meet. We do a weekly staff meeting lasting about 20 minutes with the sole purpose of praying together and putting them on the same page for what's coming up in the next few weeks. The only other meetings we have are two 3 hour staff meetings a year. In these two meeting, we go over long range planning and team building exercises.

Thirdly, do not just be a staff that meets for work. This past January I shut down every activity except for our Sunday mornings and Mid-week services. We did not meet individually or collectively for any purpose. I invited my entire staff and their families over to my house every Sunday Night in place of our evening service at church, simply for fellowship. We ate, played games, and watched the NFL playoffs. It was one of the most productive times of my ministry. It brought unity and built lots of momentum. It was important for them that I let them in my personal space.

Lastly, get in their world. I am not a computer geek by any means. But if one of my guys wants to brag about what he is doing at work, I schedule a time to go and meet him on his turf. I also check on my staff's families. Get to know your staff's kids. It is a goal of mine to have one-on-ones moving forward as family-on-family. This way we are doing life more than just ministry.

— —

I'm Not Fussing!!

➤ You know you do not love all your staff equally. Don't feel guilty or be a liar. We have to get out of this "I love you" mode. If you don't love them, don't say it. Integrity is a must in leadership, even if it's hard to digest.

➤ Be willing to call fouls when staff members get out of alignment. You have to become David, and your Goliath is gossip and complaints. Have the "stones" to sling a rock!

➤ Do not put unnecessary demands on staff that cannot contribute in certain areas. Everyone doesn't have to be at every staff meeting. Give people permission to fulfill one role of the Student Body.

➤ Never call someone Level 2 or 3 leaders. All Leadership is vital. Some just have less responsibility for the overall objectives.

➤ There are 4 stages of leadership:

    o Tell
    o Sale
    o Delegate
    o Consult

If you ever want to know how these all breakdown, I will be happy to come do a leadership development session for you! Ha!

What You Need To Do is...

➤ Evaluate your staff and break them into Level 1, 2 or 3 leaders for the Student Body.

➤ Create minimum ministry requirements for each Level of Leadership

➤ Plug ministry leadership openings into the appropriate Level and then begin recruiting with the requirements of that Level in mind

➤ Call an "All Hands on Deck" Staff meeting and announce to everyone they are to unpack the bags of the guilt trip you have had them on all this time, and give them their requirements.

➤ Do your best to place all leadership under your inner 3 as direct reports versus you as the Mouthpiece. The difference between large churches and small ones is the layers of delegation.

Chapter 7

Got a Butt?

"I have suffered the loss of all things,
and count them but as dung..."
Phillippians 3:8

Skip this chapter

I just shared the name of this chapter with my wife. Needless to say, she rolled her eyes and walked into the next room. As she was leaving she blurted out, "You are going to make people upset and they won't finish the book." Just in case she is right, please just skip this chapter. I am going to write this chapter in for the sake of those people who, like me, have a Butt in the Study Body. I give you my word. You will gain an incredible principle from this chapter if you give me the chance to explain. If you do not plan on giving me a chance, www.half.com is a great website for selling books.

Let's face it; we all have a Butt to deal with in our Student Body. There is some mom, some older volunteer, some arrogant little college grad, or deacon who is the Butt of the Student Body. It is almost as if they are snooping through the Student Body looking for opportunities to call you out to your Head. They are nice, for the most part. But they just have this anointing to be a, well, BUTT!

My first Butt (the first few years of my ministry while I was still developing) was a HUGE one! This mom kept a record of everything I did wrong or did not follow through on. Her kids were highly active in our Student Body. Those kids were amazing student leaders and were engaged with anything we were doing, whether they were good at it or not. I loved her kids. What I hated was dealing with her. She was not my biggest fan. But to her credit, she did not keep her kids away from me, ever. I'll never forget the day she called asking me for a meeting. I'm sitting on the phone, listening and rolling my eyes, while trying to plug meetings into my calendar to get so full I would not have time to meet with her. You've never been there, I'm sure. She was not going to be denied. She informed me that her husband would be attending the meeting as well. He was a quiet man (insert joke here). But he was a man of reason. The appointment was set.

As they came into my office, I did the typical "preacher thing" and used all the preacher talk, "Brother" "Sister" and "Praise the Lord" in the beginning stages of this meeting. All the while, I had a nagging pain in my gut and strong desire to hurry this along, so the Butt could take her Butt somewhere else. The Student Body Butt started our meeting this way, "Pastor Glenn, I called this meeting today because Pastor Kemp (my Head) thought it would be the best way to handle some of the issues I have had with your leadership." She went on, "I have been very frustrated over the past fews years with some of the things you have allowed to go on without an apology or additional communication to us as parents." She continues, "My husband became so tired of hearing my complaints at home that he encouraged me to begin a log of all the discrepancies I have noticed or seen in the past few years." She goes on, "I presented these pages (I said pages) to Pastor Kemp (my Head) and he refused to take them because he wanted me to give them to you in our meeting." Wait it gets better. She proceeds to reach in her bag and pull out a manila folder. She opens up her file (HER FILE!) and says, "I would like to give you this copy of 7 pages worth of discrepancies I have witnessed in your leadership over the past several years."

I'm not sure if you got that. She had a SEVEN PAGE LOG of every mistake, every rehearsal that was cancelled, every date the newsletter went out 2 days later than expected, every time I got the teens back to the church from a trip later than the itinerary stated, and every time our mid-week service let out past HER 8:15 deadlines. Seven pages accumulated over YEARS! What makes this BUTT such a HUGE ONE is the fact that she jumped right over my authority and went straight to the guy who signs my paycheck!

Fortunately, the current Butt of the Student Body is not quite as bad. The difference here is that this Butt isn't a parent, but a volunteer on staff. She volunteers to be a Butt! (I laughed out loud when I wrote that!!) My first Butt's kids moved on and graduated, so she did as well. This made room for the new Butt to take her place. Boy is this current one living up to her role in the Student Body. To be honest, I have so many stories of this Butt, it's difficult for me to pick just one story to share. Ah yes, one particular staff meeting.

It was one of my two big staff meetings for the year. I had been extremely busy in some of my traveling and I was not near as prepared for the meeting as I should have been. I got up real early that Saturday morning and heading to the office with a Starbucks and a blank meeting agenda. I sat in my office and forged out my typical meeting agenda. My agenda document consists of these three components. The first is the name of the item on the agenda. Second is the time we spend talking about that item. Third is space for any member of my staff to jot down notes or questions to ask AT THE END.

At the beginning of our staff meeting, I allow time for fellowship around light snacks. We do light snacks because I always have a family fun-time following the meeting where I provide lunch and a fun activity for the staff and their families to be a part of. As we are standing around having light snacks and fellowship time, the Butt (sounds like a gang member) comes over and informs me that we are 3 minutes passed the allotted time for fellowship and are now infringing upon our group prayer time. The Butt then proceeded to remind me, a PASTOR, of how important prayer is for us and that we should not neglect prayer. I should have known then, this meeting was headed for disaster.

We get into our meeting, and like I always do, I play a brief team building recording for the staff to take in and learn from. I do not presume to be the authority on everything leadership. This particular audio recording was from a world-renowned leader and author. This guy has a multi-million dollar leadership business and thousands of employees across the globe. At the conclusion of his lesson, I ask for questions or comments. Who do you think the first, and only, person to raise their hand was? Ding, Ding, Ding. You guessed it! The Butt did and boy did she unload on how terrible the lesson was and how irrelevant this material was to what we as a staff are facing at our church. She proceeded to let everyone know how much of a waste of time that was for her to have to endure. She then began to question me on why I thought it necessary to share the principles he laid out to us and what did I hope to achieve by having them endure this lesson.

If you know me at all, you know I am not one to take a whole bunch of crap, Butt or not. I don't care how bad your day has been, you will not turn a meeting into a side show while I'm driving. I will do it as respectfully as possible. But I will reign you in and get you back on task or ask you to be dismissed. Well, the reason I am that way today is because of the meeting that day!

She blasted the entire meeting. Nothing I brought up was planned enough. No idea I had was thought through enough. The calendar dates that conflicted with her vacation schedule were nothing more than frustration points for her. Until finally she looked up at me and asked, "When did you decide to plan this staff meeting, this morning?" Oh yes she did. She went there and nailed me right in front of my entire team. What a Butt!

As the years have gone on, her approach has not been much better with regards to how she views things. One of her family members was on my ministry team recently, as we were doing a summer youth camp. Since she had a family member on the trip, she decided it was in her best interest to call me while I was at the camp to inform me, her family member was not thrilled about her sleeping arrangements. I responded back to the Butt, "I don't particularly care how your family member feels about her sleeping arrangements. We are not here to be celebrities; we are here to minister to these kids. If you or your family member can't minister under these conditions, feel free to come and pick her up." I immediately hung up the phone and went into the shower to get ready for that nights service.

I was furious. I am slamming stuff down and talking to myself in the mirror pretending it's her face I see. I'm yelling at the mirror everything I wished I had said, but know I could have possibly lost my job over. I know you've never been there with all your halos in the closet. After I got control of myself, I realized I had to get in the right frame of mind for the service coming in the next hour and a half.

So, I jump in the shower (terrible visual I'm sure) and began praying about the service. It was hard to pray about the service because I was so distracted by the "gas" coming from the Butt! (I laughed out loud again!) So, I started telling

God what a Butt she was. Truth be told, this is exactly what I said, "God, I can't stand her. You know I am as close to hate in my heart as ever over this butthole. She is petty and stupid. I want her to go to Heaven, but she is a butthole to me. Move her to another church, Lord. Send her to the choir, if she has to stay at our church. God, the children's pastor needs a butthole like this. Kill her if you have to, God. I am just tired of dealing with this butthole!"

In a way that only He can, the Lord spoke back to my heart and said, "She's your butthole, Son. Imagine what would happen to your body if you didn't have one."

Well, I'm in the shower and I'm washing, so you can use your imagination on where I was washing about the time I'm taking a whipping from my Daddy. His loving correction sent me on a journey to understand why God always keeps a Butt in the Student Body.

Role playing of the "Butt" kind

I began to process the contribution of the butt. Frankly, the butt removes waste from the body. It is THE part of the body to remove all unnecessary matter that currently resides inside the body. Two types of food enter the body. Food the body can use as fuel now or store for later and food the body can't use or store. The primary function of the butt is to remove unneeded food called waste.

I realized something; both of these women forced me to eliminate unnecessary and wasteful ministry ideas and habits. Every time I created a meeting the Butt had to be considered. I planned events and retreats knowing full well, if I did not have my act together, the Butt of the Student Body would be staring right at me. It was the looming threat of the Butt that revealed what was wasteful, and that kept me better organized and more precise in all of my ministry pursuits.

Today, parents NEVER challenge me on my organization skills. I have newly graduated 6th graders being allowed to go on a Shabbach Retreat without parents, simply because the Student Body Butt forced me to eliminate the "crap" I use to try and pull over on people. I do not have the luxury of being "full of it" like many of my peers do. Truth be told, I owe this book to the two ladies that refused to let me get by with anything wasteful. If it wasn't for the Butt of the Student Body, I would be the stereotypical youth pastor running around the day before we leave on a trip trying to get liability release forms so teens could go. If it wasn't for the Butt, I'd be the stereotypical youth pastor running around 5 minutes before church trying to get my sermon together. If it wasn't for the Butt, I would not have the organizational integrity to travel and train other leaders on how to effectively structure their Student Body. Today, I am becoming mature enough to understand that I NEED people who will not let me get by with mediocrity.

I know you do not want to hear this, but YOU NEED A BUTT. If the Student Body you are privileged to be the Mouthpiece for is going to be healthy, you can't afford not to have a Butt. Don't make the mistake of trying to run off every Butt God brings your way. You need him or her. I've never seen a body with multiple butts, but hey maybe you have so much crap going on, God is sending extra "crap" managers your way!

What the body does if there is no rear-end
A friend of mine recently was diagnosed with a disease I had no idea existed. The name of this disease is called, Celiac Disease. According to WebMD, this disease is a digestive and autoimmune disorder that results in damage to the lining of the small intestines when foods with gluten are eaten. Severe digestive problems occur if you continue to eat gluten in your diet. It is an ugly disease that can be associated with Crone's Disease, Rheumatoid Arthritis and even Cancer of the intestine.

My friend was devastated at the diagnosis. The reason she began to have tests run to figure out what was going on was because she was having severe constipation. She tried every home remedy possible to relieve the bloating and the lack of "waste removal." This issue of constipation due to the Celiac Disease ultimately led to fecal emesis. In case you do not know what "fecal emesis" is, it is the removal fecal matter through the mouth. Let that sink in for a moment. Because of prolonged periods of bowel obstructions, the body forced the waste out of itself through the mouth!

What was once THE portal of life, nourishment and fuel has now taken on the function of a Butt for the Body. I see it all the time. Youth pastors and leaders running around and spewing "crap" for everyone else to have to clean up. They sit around spewing crap about their Head, spewing crap about their leaders, spewing crap about their small budget, and spewing crap about how toxic their teens are. I submit to you today, you have not allowed the Butt of the Student Body to function properly, thus YOU THE MOUTHPIECE, are now functioning in that role. I mean really, who wants to get good "life giving" food from someone with crap breath? I know I am being incredibly crude, but YOU HAVE TO GET THIS PRINCIPLE! Stop trying to run off the Butt, you need him or her, otherwise you become him or her. The reason you are so negative, bitter, and just plain hateful is because what you brought in as the Mouthpiece has gone through the Student Body and now it is coming back up and out of you and seems to be nothing but a HUGE WASTE of your time. You have to learn to let even the Butt have place in the Student Body.

2 Orifices, 1 Goal

I mean let's face it. Both the Butt and the Mouthpiece have the same goal in mind for the body. The issue is, you as part of the Headship, have not followed 1 Corinthians

11:29 and have not "discerned the body correctly." The Mouthpiece and the Butt of the Student Body seek to keep the body healthy, but from two different approaches. The Mouthpiece takes in the necessary and the Butt takes out the unnecessary. You have to learn how to allow him or her to function properly in the Student Body, without driving you crazy in the process. Let me give you a few suggestions to consider.

1. Identify but NEVER DECLARE who the Butt of the Body is
2. Put something in your office as a subtle reminder of the necessary role this person plays in the Student Body that will make you smile when you look at it. For me, I have a small statue of the Veggie Tales figures from Dave and the Giant Pickle movie. The giant pickle looks like a BIG GREEN TURD! It makes me smile... pray for me.
3. Place him or her in a "detail-oriented" role where he or she can run with an area of leadership that can keep them out of your hair. I mean, if something is not well organized, and they did it. Well...they will have to call themselves out publicly.
4. Send the Butt of the Student Body the itinerary or agenda early so they can peruse the document and give input in advance.

The Butt of the Student Body is of vital importance to the overall success of the alignment process. The Butt is not in rebellion or out of alignment because he or she does not agree with everything that is said or done. Don't eliminate this person, the ramifications are disastrous. Your job as part of the Headship is to find a way to effectively allow them to function in the role they place. Now let's talk about the kids!

— —

I'm Not Fussing!!
- ➤ NEVER REVEAL WHO THE STUDENT BODY BUTT IS!! Do I have to tell you why?
- ➤ Refuse to fire those people who make your leadership challenging. All you will ever be is what you are, unless someone pressures you to change.
- ➤ You don't do everything right, that's why you have waste. Give someone permission to challenge the process. Welcome debate.
- ➤ There should be an element of conflict in every staff meeting you have. When's the last time you had people disagreeing?
- ➤ Be teachable. You can learn something from anyone. Every person on this planet is your superior in something.

What You Need To Do is...
- ➤ Use this person as the face of all your organizational shaping. If you can please this person, everyone else will be a breeze to sell change to.
- ➤ Work hard to build harmony. He/she doesn't need to be your friend, nor does he/she need to be won from the dark side. He/she needs to know you are moving in lockstep for the betterment of the Student Body. My Butt is still the same one, but our relationship is much different today, because I'm a better leader.
- ➤ Paul had a thorn in his flesh, and you have a pain as a Butt. Like Paul, this will not be taken from you, so endure.

Chapter 8

Out of your belly!

"...out of his belly shall flow rivers of living water."
John 7:38

I want to get right the point of this chapter for you. All kids are not equal in the influence they carry in the Student Body, so all kids should not get equal amounts of your time and energy. I know how that sounds. I know you want to resist what I just stated. Before you go back and re-read the last chapter, give me a chance to explain this cold, but true, reality.

In almost every leadership meeting I have with senior pastors or denominational leaders, I pose this very scenario. Without exception the response has always been the exact same. See what you would do.

Suppose an investment banker comes to you with 3 investment opportunities and guarantees a 10% return on the investment you make in any of the three ventures inside of one fiscal year. He gives you a contractually binding agreement that you will indeed gain a 10% return on the investment you make. The catch, however, is there are only specific dollar amounts attached to each investment.

Investment A is a baseline investment of $20. In other words, at the conclusion of this year, your investment in

Investment A will give you a return of $2, thus giving you the sum total of $22.

Investment B is a middle investment of $200. In other words, at the conclusion of this year, your investment in Investment B will give you a return of $20, thus giving you the sum total of $220.

Investment C is a high investment of $2000. In other words, at the conclusion of this year, your investment in Investment C will give you a return of $200, thus giving you the sum total of $2200.

If you can only chose one investment to make, and they are all going to produce a 10% return, where would you make your investment?

Without exception, the latter of the three is the answer. Why? Because people instinctively want the most return possible from the investment they made. Even an initially high investment is okay with people, if they are certain to attain high return.

I share this thought with denominational leaders often because I see them making most of their investments in churches and leaders that are baseline investments. Now, that's not a haughty statement. I am just making an observation. If your investment in a 20 member church, a 200 member church, or a 2000 member is going to produce a 10% growth in the membership of the denomination, which makes the most sense? I sit in denominational business meetings and it's their baseline investment that gets all the attention. When states bring me in for training and ministry, they ask me to cater my comments to those at the baseline of youth ministry. Now I have NO problem doing that. But I want a return for my investment as well. And for me, if I'm leaving my gorgeous wife and two kids at home, I want the highest return, because I am giving my highest investment. Don't misquote me, I am not speaking about honorariums or love offerings.

The same is true for you in the Student Body. Everyone should not get equal amounts of investment or time. You should be investing the majority of your time with the Belly of the Student Body. The Belly is made up of your Student Leaders, or Core kids. It's the belly where all the food falls before it is broken down and distributed throughout the Body. It is the Belly where waste and nutrients are determined. It is the Belly where you should make your decisions. And it is the Belly where "living water" flows. The key for you immediately, is announcing who needs to "GET IN YOUR BELLY!"

Forget who they "think" they are - let them KNOW

The greatest thing you can do is tell a teen who they are. Teens (and Men) do not catch hints very well. It is your job as the Mouthpiece to declare where your students fit in the Student Body. You have to paramount duty of establishing strong men and women in this army of the Lord. The greatest thing you can do for a student, who is a leader, is make them a player in position. A sense of ownership and responsibility rises up in any person who knows they are not just a typical person, doing what typical people do.

My pastor's son, Lee, who was also the drummer in my praise band, went into the Marines just out of high school. I remember him sharing with me the feeling of being called, "Recruit" throughout his basic training. They would not dignify him by calling him by name or by Marine, because he had not proven his worth to the corp. After weeks of training, Lee and the rest of the recruits were sent into what's called, The Crucible. Days upon days, these men were forced into the worst elements possible to provide for them the most severe training possible. Upon their journey back, the marine corp had sent word to the families of these "recruits" that this would be a great day to visit. I have heard my Head speak many times of the overwhelming emotion as he saw the "recruits" coming over the hill, headed right for them. As they finished The Crucible, one of the officers came by each recruit to hand them the "Eagle Globe and Anchor," they also looked at each one of them and called them, "Marine." It is evident how much that moment meant to Lee, even today, as he tells the story of his transition from "recruit" to "marine."

That verbiage is equally important to Belly members of the Student Body. It changes a student's sense of value and ownership when you, the Mouthpiece, declare them more than a "recruit." I have two branches of Belly students in my group. The first is called, "Dodeka." The second is called, "Cadre." These two segments of the Belly of our Student Body are vital to the direction and atmosphere of our body here. I will share with you about the objectives for both of these at the conclusion of this chapter. Before I go there, I want to try and get you thinking with your Belly, not just filling it.

the head, the heart, or the belly

Most of you reading this book will agree you are a human being. Humans make decisions from one of three places, our head, our heart, or belly. The goal of this section is try and get you making decisions from your Belly of the Student Body, not your Head or Heart. In order to do that let me explain the other two decision makers first.

When you make decisions from your head, you are making decisions from an intelligence standpoint. You calculate the pros and cons. You weigh the good scenarios and the bad scenarios of this decision and make your judgment solely from those possibilities. You aren't emotional about the decision. It's simply calculation that drives the conclusion on what you should do moving forward. It's "X or O" for you. Tithing is a great example of this type of decision making. God said 10%, so that's what you do. I'm not crying about it. Pastor's guilt trip doesn't make a difference in the check you write. It is what it is.

When you make decisions from your heart, you are making decisions from an emotional standpoint. This kind of decision making is based solely out of the mood the opportunity puts you in. Preachers are great at snagging an emotional giver. Emotional decision makers usually regret decisions made after they have had time to process. They get wrapped up in the heat of a moment (good or bad) and make decisions they have to live with or go back and fix. A heart decision maker is all centered on the moment.

When you make decisions from your belly, you are making decisions from a spirit-man standpoint. You "try the spirit" to see if it's of God. Belly decisions will seek wisdom from the Head and will take an inventory of the value of this decision from the Heart, but the deciding factor will be how your Belly feels. Belly decisions aren't overly intellectual, because you instinctively understand that God forces radical faith for great rewards. Belly decisions aren't overly emotional, because you understand that you may never sleep again because of the great faith leap you are possibly going to be taking. Belly decisions are derived from a Core belief system that is deeply rooted, not in intellect or emotion, but substance and evidence of the things you are hoping for.

When I was making Washington, DC the location of our 2nd conference, I could not afford to be a head decision maker. I had no contacts in the DC area. The denomination I am affiliated with wasn't thrilled about the Myrtle Beach conference, so I knew I would get no help from them with launching DC. I didn't have enough money to keep Myrtle Beach conference up for two years, so I knew starting another in an area of the country where I had NO contacts was just plain stupid. I couldn't make a heart decision either. The thought of taking out a second mortgage to pay for this conference would have stressed me to no end. So I had to make a Belly decision. What is it that God is telling me to do. He said, "Go." So I did. DC is still my favorite conference of the four I do to this day. I have that testimony because I made my decision with my belly, not my head or heart.

When it comes to the Student Body, make decisions from the Belly. Take a poll of what your Core students think. If you are trying to change, start at the Belly. If revival is going to fall, it will come to your Belly. Jesus said, "out of your Belly flows." He is telling us that our Core is the determining factor. I want you to be smart. You need to be emotional about some things. But the essence of change will come from the Belly. All you have to do is get your Belly hungry and the rest of the Student Body will get motivated to eat, as well.

Hunger strikes

Three years ago during our 40 days of prayer and fasting, I felt like God was calling to a complete fast of nothing but fluids. Hands down it was one of the hardest, and most rewarding, things I have ever done on my faith walk. For the first several days, I was so hungry and sick. All of the toxins stored in my body were being dissolved and all of my reserves were being depleted. I was hungry and it affected everything I did.

After about a week, I lost my hunger. I could sit at restaurants with family and friends with no problem. I actually started feeling good about where I was. I remember thinking, "this is no big deal, and maybe I'll go longer." The problem was that I was only 14 days into the process.

About day 22, my hunger came back with an attitude. My body was screaming for food. Water, milk, and juices were not adequate enough to satisfy my hunger. From day 22 until day 40, I never lost my hunger. Something interesting happened to me during those 18 days that I had never felt in my body, but I had witnessed in my Student Body.

During the last 18 days of my fast, the pain of my starvation moved from being just in my belly to my entire body. It got to the place where my legs and arms were screaming out for food. My head would hurt; even my teeth would ache for something with substance to be put into my mouth. The hunger of my Belly became so great that the rest of my body began to act out in alliance for food, as well.

If you can get your Belly hungry, sooner or later the rest of the Student Body will cry out as well. You don't need revival to hit your youth group, school, or church. You need your Belly to go on a hunger strike. If you can ever get your Belly screaming for revival, the rest of the Student Body will follow suit.

When your Belly is flabby

If your Belly is too flabby it may because you are not working them hard enough. One of the greatest mistakes I see in Student Bodies with regards to students is the lack of opportunities for them to lead. I can't count how many youth praise teams I watched full of adults. Youth drama teams have adult leads. All the stages at conferences are filled with adults leading teens. I understand the principle behind it all. I just think it is incredibly weak minded of a Student Body to have no place for students to lead.

They are too immature. They lack spiritual depth. They are closet sinners. They are sleeping with their girlfriend. They don't know enough scripture. I've heard it all, and they are understandable reasons for not including students in the leadership of the Student Body. The difference for me is I expect teenagers to act like teenagers. I think we put way too many stipulations on students these days to be active in leadership in the Student Body. I want saved students leading the way. I want students striving for spiritual depth. I don't want student leaders sleeping with their boyfriend. I want my students to have all of Psalms memorized. Truth is half of my staff, and half of the people reading this book, were well into their late 20's before they met these requirements, if at all. Cut kids some slack and give them some leadership. The greatest thing they could ever do is feel the weight of a children's Sunday school class lesson. For real, how saved do they need to be to do puppets? I'm not promoting hypocrisy; I'm promoting growth by trial and error with permission to be an immature student, who has leadership duties.

I used to be extremely dogmatic in my approach of this issue. I was raised very legalistic. All that changed when Richard, my bass player, came to me about wanting to learn how to play the bass and playing it for the worship team. Now before you call me a sell out for talent, Richard was a 15 year old kid who had never played a day in his life when he asked me. Richard was an angry kid, who didn't really fit in the Student Body anywhere. He kind of hung out on the edge of the Student Body and refused to connect. He showed up every week, only because his parents made him. He didn't like church, he didn't like God, and half the time he hated me. So here is this angry kid who doesn't even like church asking me if could he play an instrument he had never played, for a band at a church he didn't like, for a God he was not in a relationship with. Intellectually, it was a no-brainer. Emotionally, I didn't really like the kid either. But my Belly said this was my last chance to win him to the Body of Christ. So, I let him join under the condition he kept his bass turned off until he could actually play. He would just play away with no volume. It was funny.

After many years and battles, I saw joy come. Jesus became the passion and pursuit of his life. This once angry kid, who wanted nothing to do with God or church, now is a key leader in the Shoulders of our Student Body and a key leader for our Shabbach Conferences.

Richard was just the beginning of this Belly training model for our Student Body. Today, I develop groups of

Belly students at a time through my two branches called, "Cadre and Dodeka."

Cadre is my discipleship track. In this track, some of my key Shoulders focus on developing the "Life of the Student Body." Cadre focuses on developing a well-rounded Christian life for student leaders through the six practices of spiritual disciplines.

1. A Prayer Life
2. Life in the Word
3. Devotional Life
4. Life with the Body
5. Meditation Life
6. Life in the "Fast" Lane

I would go into a brief overview of each of these, but this will be the basis for my next book.

Dodeka means the number 12, in the Greek. This is a high impact leadership group, led by one of my inner 3. The purpose of this group is to walk with 12 student disciples and help shape them into the leaders of the Student Body today, and the leaders of the church, tomorrow. This group is brought together with the purpose of developing strong, spiritual disciples who understand servant leadership.

The student leaders of Cadre and Dodeka have exclusive access to me and upcoming information with where the direction of our Student Body is heading. These young lions and lionesses are at the forefront of change and decision making. You come into our Student Body and you see Belly before you see Body, and I LOVE IT THAT WAY!!

I'm Not Fussing!!

> ➤ Students do not have to be perfect in order to be used, so don't put that pressure on them. You are flawed. You have bad days and act dumb sometimes. Let teenagers be teenagers, without penalty.
> ➤ Your Belly is where the majority of your time should be invested. These students should get the best of your time, not what's left of it.
> ➤ Grow as a leader to the point you are more proactive in leadership development and less reactive in pastoral care emergencies.

What You Need To Do is...

> ➤ Endorse struggling student leaders. If a student leader is struggling, they are trying. That is not the moment to boot them off the worship team or drama. Get real. When can the church go back to being a place where sick people don't have to pretend they are not?
> ➤ Clearly define the criteria for student leadership in the Student Body and begin highlighting those students with roles to play each week. From altar workers and greeters to ushers and puppeteers, find ways for them to take active leadership roles in the lives of their peers and young children
> ➤ Get as many student leaders as possible, who sense a call into ministry, to begin teaching young children. If they can learn to communicate now, what will they become when they have the integrity to house the calling?

Chapter 9

Legs Stuck to the Pew!

"then Jesus said to him,
"Get up! Pick up your mat and walk."
John 5:8

I made a terrible mistake early on in my Student Body. I had the privilege of being the student pastor to a great kid. For the sake of the book, let's call him, Tom. Tom was from a great family with a great financial means. What was most impressive about Tom was, he was the most humble and helpful student I had ever met. He also happened to drive multiple high-end cars. When I needed to move from Charlotte to Fort Mill, Tom was there from start to finish helping me unload. Tom simply enjoyed being around me and asking for my input in his life. What was most amazing about Tom was he would actually implement the insight and completely change things in his life based upon what I would say to him, no matter what the suggestion would be. If I needed to repaint an area of the Family Life Center, Tom was there. If I had a late night hospital run or party to bust up into, Tom was right beside me. Tom was a great guy and everyone loved the element Tom brought to the table.

As Tom got older, I had a revelation of grooming him to become one of the three components of the Neck of my Student Body. I started pushing Tom into leadership positions. I would force him in front of an audience and push him to lead. The terrible mistake was, I was forcing him into a position of leadership. Tom was (and is) a great guy, but he is not a leader. Tom can work circles around people and is one of the smartest people I know. He has incredible insight and was the only person for years that pushed me to innovative thoughts during brainstorming sessions. I forced Tom into leadership, but Tom was not a leader.

It came from the right motives in my heart. I knew Tom had my heart, and I knew he had the ability to take an order. The mistake came when I tried to push him to give orders when he did not have the skills to lead. He was a great guy, just not a leader.

I watched him become more and more miserable. I watched those I forced under his leadership become more and more miserable. I thought I could coach him into leadership. I thought I could teach him to do it like me. The issue was, Tom had my style. Tom had my catch phrases. Tom had my facial expressions. Tom had my excel spreadsheets and event checklists. It was the thing Tom did not have that killed him in leadership positions. Tom DID NOT have my ability to lead. Tom was a great follower, but a terrible leader.

Tom eventually quit the Student Body. I became so frustrated and argumentative, the great parts of who he was became peripheral qualities to the negative, bitter guy he was. This mistake proved to be the death of his involvement in the Student Body and our relationship. He still attends our church. He still is an incredible guy. Even today, I see him vacillating between servant roles and leadership ones. It hurts my heart a little, because I put the thrill of leading in him, even though that's not his gifting.

The day I left for the beach to come finish this book, I popped my head in my executive pastor's office. Sitting on his desk was a resignation letter from Tom in an area of our adult church body, which he was leading. Tom is an incredible gift to our church. Tom in the right servant role position will take our church body beyond what we as pastors can imagine. The key is knowing everyone is not a leader, and that it doesn't make them less important.

Fact is...

Face the facts; every student is not going to be a leader. However, every student is important to the overall functioning of the Student Body. You need "file and rank" students in the Student Body as much as you need Belly students. They do not have to be a leader to be effective. Some students are called to maintain motion, not instigate it.

Imagine our United States Army filled with 5 Star Generals. No one is a lieutenant. No privates. No sergeants. No corporals. We have an army filled with generals. Nothing would ever get done because everyone would be giving orders and no one would be there to take the orders given.

I was asked in a "question and answer" leadership session a couple weeks ago to define a student leader. I love getting questions thrown at me off the cuff. Most guys get nervous or carry the pressure of trying to sound profound. Not me. I carry a label of being clever and witty.

As a matter of fact, my senior year of college, I was tied in votes with my best friend, now brother in-law, for the "wittiest" is male in our college. People call it, "Witty." I call it "Stating the obvious."

I immediately responded to the question this way:

"The definition of a student leader is a student who has followers."

You are blown away by that revelation aren't you? See how clever and witty I am. You, like the group at the leadership session, were expecting this deep revelation of the role and significance of a Student Leader in the Student Body.

You wanted me to unpack this magnificent concept from the deep wells of the infallible Word of God. You, like them, wanted me to illuminate the relationship of Timothy to Paul in the world of student leadership and cast upon you the transforming power that comes from a renewed mind.

Sorry. I'm not that profound.

However, there is a profound truth to still be had, even in the obviousness of the answer I gave. A student leader is a student who has FOLLOWERS. The fact is, even if everything from the Belly up is healthy and functioning, you are still in a paralyzed state because you have no ability to create motion. Followers produce leaders, not the other way around. Followers also produce motion towards or away from a specific direction. Your Student Body will be led by your Belly, but it will actually move in the direction your Student Body's legs are going.

The Student Body is strengthened by the Belly. Hunger strikes the Student Body from the Belly. However, movement is created and sustained in the Legs of the Student Body.

Legs in motion

The Legs of the Student Body is the area you have to stretch. Simply put, they contain your largest muscles necessary for significant movement. In other words, this is where real power is generated. The followers, sometimes called regular attendees, really put the muscle behind anything going on in the Student Body. The Mouthpiece speaks direction. The Neck makes the deposit of that direction and creates the shift for the Student Body to see from a new direction. The Shoulders lug the weight of the direction shift. Your Belly generates passion for shifting. But it is the Legs of the Student Body that have the sheer muscle to get it moving in that direction. Don't ever underestimate the power of a follower. They do what they are. They follow.

If the Legs of your Student Body are "stuck in the pew," it's not their fault. If the Legs seem paralyzed and unmovable, it's not from the absence of power. Motionless Legs are the result of signals not reaching them. I hear peers of mine fuss and complain all the time about their Student Body not having the power to do go anywhere other than where they have always been. Pardon my language, "BULL DOOKIE!" You have had the power for movement all along; your issue is that the Legs aren't getting the signal communicated to them.

A very special man in our church was diagnosed a few years back with ALS, also known as Lou Gehrig's Disease. Bottom line, it's the slow deterioration of muscles in the body.

Larry is an unbelievable man of prayer. When he contracted this disease our church family was shaken, but I saw him strengthened through this process.

As the years have gone on, and ALS has slowly been breaking down his body, Larry has lost all movement in his arms and partially in the muscles in his mouth. When he was diagnosed with this disease he begged God for one thing, not to allow this disease to keep him from being able to stand for worship. After several years past the life expectancy of someone with ALS, Larry walks into church under his own strength and stands as long as every healthy man and woman in the church during worship. How can he do that, you ask? Well, the signals from his head to his arms aren't working, so they do not move. But the signal from his head to his legs is flowing just fine. Because that signal has always been fine, his muscles in his legs have the power to sustain movement. That sustaining movement has kept the muscles in his legs from deteriorating. The lack of deterioration is what keeps his body moving, in spite of his arms inability to function.

Your inability to move is not because of the Legs, the students who follow and just attend, but is a reflection of communication that is not flowing down beyond the Belly. Followers follow. If they aren't moving, it's because someone directly above them is not leading. If you can find the breakdown in leadership, you can get movement. I'm not talking about traction, I'm speaking about movement. We will deal with traction in the next chapter.

The Legs are vital indicators of leadership. It's in the Legs where you find out what type of leadership you have in you, and the type of leadership you have around you. There is not a whole lot you can do to keep Legs in alignment. They do what they are "signaled" to do. If they aren't doing anything, then it shows one of two things happening above them in leadership.

First, their inactivity could be revealing a breakdown in communication. Somewhere above them the signal got dammed up. This is very important for you to trace down. Remember the goal here. When the oil hits the bottom of the garment, the commanded blessing is released. We are after the blessing. Don't lose sight of the overall objective here. If someone is damming the flow because of lack of communication, you have to fix the connection.

This especially important because you know how petty students can be. Let someone cheat on someone. Let someone break up with their boyfriend. Let someone put a crude remark about someone else on facebook. Let some girl wear something weird on Easter Sunday and get made fun of. Any of these petty things can be the proverbial "scissor to the wire" of the flow. Your job is to seek out the communication break and fix it, not the drama that caused it.

Or secondly, and more severe, their inactivity could reveal a rebellion against the direction the Student Body is trying to go. You MUST find this and remove the dam being built. It may be that you have to fire a volunteer or remove an element of leadership. Either way you have to deal with the dam. It is blocking your ability to move. By "it" I mean he, she or they. You must be willing to confront rebellion.

I know confrontation is not fun. If you enjoy confrontation, you have a few issues a counselor needs to help you navigate through. I do not enjoy conflict, but I will confront quickly any conflict I deem as a possible rebellion against the aligning of the Student Body. Just because I am quick to confront, does not in any way mean I enjoy it. To be honest I hate it. But the thought of what will never happen is scarier to me than the threat of losing a staff member or student.

I am after the commanded blessing for the Student Body. I am after an anointing and calling on a generation that this planet has never seen since its foundation was established. I want to see a generation deeply rooted and established in the things of God. I want more than anything to see a Student Body rise up in unity to operate in so much blessing, so much favor, and so much anointing that a town, city, region, state, and nation will be changed. I believe that is a small glimpse into what the commanded blessing has for a Student Body in spiritual alignment.

That blessing is worth asking a rebellious staff to go sing in the choir. Lucifer was the choir director in heaven, so it's only fitting that a demon in the Student Body should be cast into the place where Satan reigns at every church! I was just kidding Music pastors. Get a life, I was joking around, sort of.

Seriously, I am after the commanded blessing. Losing a student to another church is okay with me in light of the blessing. Having adults who do not like our Student Body doesn't trouble me at night, when I am focused on the commanded blessing. If my ego is in the way, I have a real problem with these people, personally. If my ego is in the way, I will feel the need to defend myself or fight for the honor of the Student Body. If my ego is in the way, I will raise my voice or lose my cool. If my ego is in the way, I think their rebellion is against me, not the aligning for the Blessing.

Don't make it personal, because it's not. It's about the Body being aligned so the oil can get to the bottom so the blessing can be commanded. In any conflict where you are addressing rebellion, unity demands you never use words like I, me, my, or mine. THIS IS NOT ABOUT YOU. This person doesn't even really know you. Stay focused on the alignment, so the oil can flow and the blessing can be commanded.

Applauding the right behavior

I spent the majority of this chapter talking to you about what the Legs of the Student Body indicates more than what the Legs need in order to stay in alignment. Aside from getting the signal communicated down to them, I want to finish this chapter with the one major principle you as the Mouthpiece must apply to keep the Legs of the Student Body moving in the right direction.

Your Legs (followers or regular attendees) know they are moving in the right direction when you are continuously applauding the right behavior. You taking the time to applaud the right behavior is more "movement" critical than "mission' critical. This will be a big paradigm shift for a lot of you reading this book because of how you were brought up in church.

I was raised with two things hanging over my head in every church setting: #1 was the rules and #2 was the consequences of breaking those rules. I was taught the right way to do things by being punished for doing them in the wrong manner first. Can you identify? Granted, I deserved the majority of the punishment I received. I was what they called a "hellion" for any Sunday school teacher or pastor to deal with. One of my crowning achievements growing up was when I made a Sunday school teacher quit teaching. The day she retired, she looked at me and said she was quitting because she could not take 2 more years of dealing with me in the high school class. I know, I know. I was awful, but now she loves me and is proud of me! That has to count for something, right?

I believe the approach to your Legs should be the opposite of my upbringing. I have noticed my most productive discipling comes through applause more than correction. The majority of what students do is for attention anyway. The way they dress, the way they act, the things they take part in, and the things they refuse to engage in are all driven by attention. So many Mouthpieces spend the majority of their energy aligning the Student Body through fixing bad behavior. The problem with this method is you have very little time to nurture those operating correctly. I believe the greatest way to align your Student Body is by relentlessly applauding appropriate behavior.

In every worship service I focus on the students who are doing right. If you want my attention, you have to be operating in alignment. The worshippers are celebrated, instead of the dead-heads being chastised. The students who come down front to worship are engaged with, instead of the apathetic up against the back wall being begged to be a part. The students taking notes during the sermon are rewarded versus the kid texting and having his phone confiscated. The students who come to the altar for prayer get my full attention during the altar time, not me standing up there begging basketball players who can't wait for the service to end, to come and pray first. We use our energy to applaud those who are aligned, versus wasting energy on those who refuse to be connected to the body. Why? The right applause for the right behavior keeps the Student Body moving in the right direction. Ultimately, that's what we want. Try and stay away from negative reinforcement to produce the right behavior. It's the long way to alignment.

Once we get the Student Body moving, we need to make sure we have traction. The only way to get traction is to make sure a portion of the Student Body is on the ground. Brace yourself, here comes the smelly feet!

— —

I'm Not Fussing!!

➢ Stop calling apathy out from the pulpit! For every kid sitting or doing something wrong, I bet there are 5 doing the right thing. Learn to see the good and ignore the bad. When you highlight the wrong behavior, you are *highlighting* the **WRONG** behavior.

➢ Demonstrate yourself what you are looking for. If you are looking for worshippers, be one. If you are looking for people to say, "Amen" to you, say it yourself on Sunday. I wonder what kind of audience member you are to your Head. Maybe your apathetic students are just reflections of you…

➢ Make room for non-leaders to have roles they can buy into.

What You Need To Do Is…

➢ Learn to give students the choice. When students choose correctly and act accordingly, give them the reward of your full attention. If a student who has been completely engaged in worship and Word needs me immediately following the service, they get all of me. Students who aren't engaged may only get a hug. I do not have the energy to expend on people who aren't actively involved in where we are going as a Student Body. Those outside the Student Body get what is left of me, not my best.

➢ Begin making assessments of students in the Legs that have Belly potential. Everyone can't be a leader; it would be chaos. When you do find those that are untapped, begin issuing high challenges for them to step up and engage.

➢ Begin shifting your messages to ownership of God's campus, not attendance. Those who can step up, will.

➢ Find responsibilities for non-leader students to begin contributing. You don't need a leader to set up chairs or put out Bibles.

Chapter 10

Duh Huh, It's what Feet are for

"that went down to the skirts of his garments."
Psalm 133:2b

If you are just tuning in, allow me to bless you with some personal information, I hate feet. I think feet are the worst part of the body, and I want you to know that upfront so you have the foundation for why this story is so important for me to share with you.

I took all 17 members of my student worship band to a music conference held in Orlando, FL a few years back. Orlando is an 8 hour drive from Charlotte. We took our 15 passenger white GMC church van and also rented a white Ford Expedition for the journey. I drove the 7 seater expedition full of teenagers and we placed the luggage in the additional seating in the van. We were having a blast on the way down..

I am the scariest driver a student has ever met. No one sleeps when I'm driving. There is no guarantee when I will strike, but it is guaranteed that I will strike. One moment cruising smoothly down the interstate, the next minute slamming on brakes and faking a 10 car pile-up to freak-out any snoozing teens. I don't have the privilege to travel with my team like that very often anymore due to the nature of my

139

ministry in this particular season, but this trip was one of the most memorable.

It is an established rule in my Student Body that I HATE FEET! I don't like them. I hate looking at them. My statement is, "Do not put your pickles near me!" I call them pickles because when feet begin to sweat they carry a sour smell like vinegar. I can't say, "Get your vinegar away from me." That's not even close to "clever."

Anyway, there is a beautiful young girl in my youth group named, Sherra. Sherra was sitting in the middle of the second row of the Expedition. She was a wonderful member of our Student Body and a key leader for us in the Belly position. My only complaint in regards to Sherra was the 5 "fingers" she had on each foot. Yes, I said it correctly. Her toes looked like 5 long digits that she could spread out and manipulate one by one like fingers! I hate feet regardless, but hers were just plain nasty to look at! Her peers in the youth group would call her, "Monkey feet."

Our drive to Orlando was filled with singing and gesturing to truck drivers to blow their horns at us. I was having a great time, but I did not realize there was a mutiny brewing aboard the Expedition. As I continued singing and gesturing, the rest of the team began influencing Sherra to take her shoes off and stick her monkey feet in my face! I'm nauseated right now as I reflect back.

We had been on the road for several hours and finally hit the Florida line just near Jacksonville. We decided to stop at Burger King to get a bite to eat and stretch our legs. As I pulled into the parking spot, the most disgusting object passed in front of my face. You guessed it. Monkey feet came to pinch my nose! Up until this point, people assumed I was just joking about hating feet as much as I said. But the account of what happened next has been told and retold for generations of students in hopes that they will never fall prey to stupidity as Sherra did that day.

Before I could process what happened, my "flight or fight" instincts kicked in. Like a tiger backed into a corner, I whirled around to Sherra, claws up ready to strike. As I turned, words flooded out of my mouth like someone with food poisoning purging their system. "I don't know what you were thinking. But if you ever put your nasty, cankered, monkey feet near me again, I am going to knock your head off! I don't hit girls but I will render you unconscious. I know I will lose my job, but I don't care you nasty little girl with hobbit feet. You better get out of the SUV right now before I do something I will enjoy and you will have to go to therapy to resolve!"

No one knew what to say. Silence blanketed the vehicle. Quietly, one by one they filed out to walk into the restaurant. Emily, my wife, came up and said, "Glenn you were way too cruel to her. You need to..." But before my beautiful wife could finish her statement. I interrupted her and said, "That was ridiculous and I am not going to apologize. You know how I am about feet. If God wanted feet in my face, He would have put them where my ears are."

No matter how terrible that story was and no matter how big of a jerk you think I am, the truth is Feet were made for the floor. They work best at ground level. Feet should not be propped up for long periods of time. Feet should be in contact with the earth. That is why God did not place them on the head.

No matter the motion made, it is all for naught if you do not progress on the ground level. The key for any Body, especially the Student Body, is to start walking. All the alignment and all the effort is all a waste if it does not get to the ground level. Your Head can produce the signals. You, the Mouthpiece, can provide the fuel necessary. The Shoulders can load up the supplies. The Belly can distribute the desire. The Legs can create the movement. But the Student Body does not gain an inch of ground until the Feet make an impact on ground level.

You can't afford to get everyone aligned but stop at the legs. If you have worked for the unification of the Student Body all the way through to the Legs, don't stop now. You are too close to the blessing. As promised in Psalm 133, it took the oil getting all the way down to the Feet before it was commanded.

Where the Blessing is commanded

The blessing comes when you are unified all the way to Feet of the Student Body. The Feet represent newcomers to the Student Body. They can be first time visitors or students that have been coming for a couple months to check things out. How they enter into the Student Body determines the imprint you are making in the world around you.

When you put your feet on the scales, that contact determines the weight of the body. Your imprint in the world around you and the weight of your Student Body is revealed by the contact of the Feet at ground level.

The Feet are the thermometer by which you can gauge your level of effectiveness in the schools, towns, and communities you are ministering to. If you do not properly take care of and draw in newcomers, you are "shooting yourself in the foot." I know it was a cheesy wordplay, but the point of this principle is poignant. You must begin collecting data about the imprint your Feet are making in your community.

The imprint lets you know the depth of your Student Body. It tells you the width of the Student Body's structure. It also reveals the length of the Student Body's influence in the community at large. Take an inventory. See what ethnicity you are reaching. Notice what age group you are reaching. What are the schools you are reaching? What type of student is being attracted to you? All of these are important for you to know because it shows you what leadership area is making the most impact. The one making the most impact should garner the majority of you and your resources.

Flexology

Not only are your Feet the determining factor for the level of imprint you are making around you, but it is also an indicator for what is happening beneath the skin.

Once a year, I go to a store in the Potomac Mills Mall in Woodbridge, VA called, Healthwise. Healthwise is a massage place filled with oriental men and women who market a physical assault, as a massage. Just so we are clear. I am not a pampered chef. I have never had a mani/pedi, nor do I ever plan on having one. I do not do massages. It's something about people being in my personal space, all up on me that makes me very uncomfortable, unless it's my wife. You can get a massage at Healthwise and still remain fully clothed. After 3 conferences, my body is exhausted, so I force myself to have a 45 minute massage.

The last time I went to Healthwise, I opted for an hour session. About 45 minutes in, Samurai Sam decides to massage my feet. Have I told you how much I hate feet? I don't even like my own, and I especially hate someone messing with them. I don't speak Chinese, and Samurai Sam wasn't fluent in English, so I couldn't stop him. But the longer he went, the more tingling I felt throughout my entire body. I had a headache when I entered Healthwise. As he was working on my feet, my headache disappeared.

When I got off the table, I went over to the entrance and read the promotional material on what they called Flexology. The basic synopsis of Flexology is, virtually all of your nerve endings are in your feet. Certain points throughout your feet can have specific effects on vital organs. Flexology simply states, "Every vital organ in your body has a direct root of connection inside your feet." I knew then, I was on to something.

If Flexology is adaptable into our theology, this means
the function of our heart and every other vital organ we
can't see on the surface has a strong connection with the
Feet of the Student Body. If you want to work on your heart,
mess with the Feet. If you want to see how the pancreas and
liver are functioning, mess with the Feet. Bottom line, the
Feet are great indicators of what lies beneath the surface in
the Student Body.

Once you have collected the data from the imprint you
are making on ground level, balance that data against the
intelligence you received about the vital organs inside the
Student Body. Based upon these two reports, you will have
to determine what to do with the data you like and the data
you don't like. My suggestion is to take a page out of Jesus'
Book and shake the dust from your feet!

Shake the dust baby

One snare you will have to guard with all diligence is
your Feet's direct connection to the world. **Oil runs from
the Head to the Feet of the Student Body, but the dirt we
deal with in the Student Body comes from the ground, up.**
Jesus is explicit in Matthew 10:14 when He says, "If anyone
will not welcome you or listen to your words, *shake the dust
off your feet* when you leave that home or town." When I say
"shake the dust" I am referring to you guarding the balance
between making an impact in your world through the movement of the Student Body and allowing the Student Body to
kick up the dirt in a way that the dirt can become attached.
Our bodies are made from dust, so I am not bashing anyone
who isn't in the Body of Believers. We all started there ourselves. What I am noticing is this desire to BE dirty in order
to make an imprint in the dirt.

In your venture to make a significant impression in the
world around your Student Body, do not allow the tempta-
tion to "be all things to all people" dictate the desire to be

a standout in your community. The worst thing you can do in aligning of the Student Body is to make it a place where everyone fits. This is a paradigm shift for a lot of us in ministry, because we are out to win everyone. The goal of THE CHURCH is to win everyone, but it is not the goal of the Student Body you are the mouthpiece for. In other words, everyone should be welcome to try your Student Body at Feet level, but in no way should <u>everyone</u> fit into it for a long time.

The current journey God has me on deals with this very issue in my life. I have been so focused on winning everybody; my ministry resembles any other Student Body you can find. Oh, we may sing different and I may preach different, but it is basically the same product in different packaging. It's kind of like choosing the prescription or getting the generic. They both function for the same purpose. The choice is made by the price the customer is willing to pay. I do not think this should be the case in the Student Body. What we have is not consumable, so we are not winning consumers. Instead we are to be consumed, so *we* must be the sacrifice.

To be very plain with you, a Baptist kid should not fit real well in a Charismatic Student Body long term. A Pentecostal kid should not fit in a Catholic Student Body long term. But most of all, someone who is not in an authentic relationship with Christ should not be comfortable in any spiritually aligned Student Body long term. I, in NO WAY, am endorsing one denomination over another. If you believe Jesus is THE Christ, THE son of THE Living God, you and I have common ground. I have determined to "Major on the Majors" in theological debates. However, I do have a stance on what I believe the Scriptures to mean concerning major divisions in THE Body of Christ. If you see me in a conference or listen to my podcast, you will see I have an opinion. And with fear and trembling before the God I will answer to one day, I will openly declare that opinion in the right setting. So in essence, I force you into making a decision about the Gospel I present. Everyone will not agree or like what I say. Everyone is not going to appreciate my candid, almost crude, approach to presenting truth. I may not be spiritually gifted enough for the charismatic. I may not be calm enough for the Baptist. I may not be religious enough for the catholic. I may not be dogmatic enough for the Pentecostal. But I am who I am. The Student Body I am leading is who we are. We don't look like any other Student Body in the nation. So when a speck of dust attaches to the Feet, it has a choice to make rather quickly. You, like all of us at the moment of conversion, have to choose to no longer be a speck of dust and choose to be made into the image and likeness of God by finding alignment in this Student Body or we will "shake the dust from our Feet."

As famous as Paul is for admonishing us to "be all things," he is also known for reminding us, "this ONE THING I DO." I don't want a Jack in the Box Student Body, where we are pretty good at doing a bunch of options. I believe each Student Body is called to be "Just Chicken" in their approach to imprinting the world around them. Every time you "shake the dust" and dirt flies out of your group, do not be discouraged. Let it be a reminder that you have been unique in your Student Body approach and everyone isn't going to stay attached. Those people not attaching doesn't mean you are doing something wrong, it may simply mean you are being true to yourself, and they are not right for this Body.

That tension leads me to the next chapter. There are some areas of the Student Body I cannot address. Not because they are not important, rather, they will be unique to the demographics of your area and the focus of your mission. So let's go there in "Not Going There!" haha

— —

I'm Not Fussing!!

➤ Have the courage to be distinctive in your approach to the Student Body's role in your community. This means you must not compete with other churches in your community.

➤ Have the courage to let students leave who cannot fit in the Student Body. It's a sign you have a niche in the student ministry market.

➤ Have the courage to send students to other Student Bodies; allow them to see if the grass truly is "greener on the other side." This will help you with getting spoiled students over being ungrateful. Either they realize how blessed they are, or they leave. Either way, problem solved.

What You Need To Do is...

➤ Read the book, "The Collapse of Distinction" by Scott McKain

➤ Evaluate what types of students visit your Body. This will help you understand what type of Student Body you are.

➤ Evaluate what types of students do not stay. This will help you know what you are not.

➤ Find "This one thing you do" and stay in your sweet spot.

➤ Do a study of the types of students you have currently in the Student Body to gain a clear understanding of what the Body looks like. What is the dominant gender? What is the average age? What is the student to staff member ratio? How many races are affiliated? What types of students dominate the Body? (Skater/Redneck/Prep/Rich/Poor/etc)

Chapter 11

Not going there!

"There are some things in them that are
hard to understand…"
2 Peter 3:16

I f you are like me, you have been reading this book wondering about the obvious parts of the Student Body I have
yet to address. Well, I'm not going there with you. My reason
being because the obvious parts I feel like are missing in this
book are parts that vary based upon who you are, where your
Student Body is located geographically, and what type of
vision your entire church body carries.

What I will attempt to do is address some thinking points
for you to ponder in three of the areas of the Student Body
I have yet to address. Those three areas that are obvious,
in my opinion, are the Student Body's arms, reproductive
organs, and heart. For me to not address each of these in a
specific chapter is in no way trying to say they are not important. Rather, these areas of the Student Body are so specific
to the overall identity of each Student Body, I do not believe
one person can make a broad stroke and fit every Student
Body into a cookie-cutter mold.

I believe the Arms are symbolic of the goals you, as the
Student Body, hope to reach and attain. I believe what you
reproduce through your Student Body is specific to the Body,

itself. I believe the Heart of the Student Body will be focused on the overall mission of the Body of Christ, but manifested in a particular way by your Student Body that will be unique from any other. Let me give you some things to "ponder in your heart," like Mary the mother of Jesus, in each of these very important areas of the Student Body.

within arm's reach

The reason I do not address the arms in this book is they represent the attaining of the prize (goals) you are stretching for. I can't deal with the goals for your Body. Goals for each Student Body will vary due to size, geography, and purpose. What I would like to do is share with you seven keys to attaining the goals you put forth for your Body to reach with its Arms. If this were merely a Leadership Blog or leadership session at a conference, I would entitle this, "How to "C" the Goal Fulfilled. haha

Key 1: Make the Goal CLEAR

Be sure that the goal the Arms are reaching for is a clearly defined one the entire Student Body understands. Most Student Bodies randomly shoot in the air until something is hit and falls. Once it falls and is found, the leaders run over and draw a target on the object and declare, "I meant to do that!" You are a liar and the truth ain't in you.

Key Question: Does everyone in the Student Body know what is most important?

Key 2: Get COMMITTED to the Goal

In goal achievement, it is critical that the Student Body is actually committed to attaining the clearly defined goal. Lip service will never attain the goal. You need people who are on board and ready to progress.

Key Question: Does the Student Body as a whole want to do it?

Key 3: Make sure the Goal CONVERTS

You will need to be specific and strategic on how this Goal is implemented throughout the Student Body. In your initial presentation of the Goal, be sure to show how each branch of the Student Body will be impacted in a positive way when the Goal is obtained. Also be sure to articulate how each branch can strive for the Goal. You will need to articulate to each branch of the Student Body things they are currently doing that they can stop, and things they need to begin in order to achieve the Goal.

Key Question: Does the Student Body know how to make the Goal happen in their specific area of the Body?

Key 4: Make sure you COMMISSION the Goal

It is very important that you enable your Student Body to accomplish the Goal. I do not mean make easy Goals important. I mean divide important Goals into easy steps. Nothing inspires people to action like breaking a God-sized dream out into Man-sized steps. Otherwise, it is so lofty no one feels like the effort is worth the risk.

Key Question: How do I make it easier for the Student Body to attain the Goal?

Key 5: Make sure your Goal forces COLLABORATION

One key element in any organization is synergy. In order to keep synergy in the Student Body, you must make sure the Goal laid before them is something toward which everyone needs to run. Silos are glaringly obvious in the Student Body. We preach unity, but never have it. I believe one of the major reasons for this is that we do not set Goals everyone feels they can play a key part in achieving. Another major reason we lack collaboration is because only the Headship gets credit. Work hard to get collaboration and spread around the praise.

Key Question: Is the entire Student Body working effectively towards the Goal?

Key 6: Make the Goal in a way that people can be CHARGED

Accountability will be the lynchpin for attaining the Goal. You can *expect* what you are willing to *inspect*. As the Mouthpiece, you role does not stop after you have declared the Goal. You must come back and be able to "Charge" someone who did not follow through on the commitment they made toward achieving the Goal. There is only one thing worse than having someone drop the ball when you are depending on them… that is not holding the person accountable. Sanctioned incompetence is demoralizing to your whole Body. It is your job to hold people responsible.

Key Question: Is the Student Body leadership reporting to each other on their progress?

Key 7: CELEBRATE incrementally when the Student Body is progressing towards the Goal

The 7 Days of Creation is the biblical illustration of this key. God, the Father's ultimate Goal was to make sure the heavens and the earth were completely assembled. But at the conclusion of each day, He stopped and had a celebration. In incremental steps, He would stop and pat Himself on the back and say, "It is good." The same is true of the Student Body as you progress towards your Goal.

Key Question: At the completion of what stages in route to the overall Goal, can the Student Body pause to celebrate?

These keys are "Key" in setting up your Goals for the Student Body. If you will take the time to pray and plan before you ever reveal the Goal, you will be amazed at how cohesive the Student Body will be. What Goals you determine to go after are based upon where you are and what type of Student Body you have. These keys to setting Goals for the Student Body's Arms to reach towards apply, no matter what your demographics are.

shhhh...it's private
Those of you who know me, expected me to deal with reproduction. Sorry to disappoint you, but it's really not something I can align for you with regards to the Student Body. I know every Body has the organs for reproducing. Every Body is supposed to reproduce. I also believe that it will take another Student Body who is opposite in your particular approach to connect with, in order for real reproduction to take place. However, most Student Bodies are so insecure in themselves; they could never connect with another Student Body in the same town to spawn reproduction. This lack of connection to another Student Body is why we aren't really reproducing, but we should save this thought for another time.

God, all the way in the beginning, looked at Adam and said, "BE FRUITFUL AND MULTIPLY..." It's a mandate for every Student Body. The fact remains; you don't really control what is produced from the act of reproduction. Understanding this, I would like to give you some "ambiance" principles to think about, and then explain why you can't force specifics in reproduction.

Ambiance Principle 1 – Atmosphere is critical in the reproductive process.

The right atmosphere is crucial in the reproductive process. The mood you set in your classes, small groups, or services will be big motivating factors in the process. Music played, songs sung, presentations, lighting, and drama will draw people into the mood or push them away. The atmosphere necessary will be conditional to your area and style of ministry. Whatever the case, just make sure you have a strategic plan to ensure the atmosphere is correct for reproduction in the Student Body.

Ambiance Principle 2 – There must be a removal of clothing

In other words, vulnerability is very important in reproduction. Every facet of the Student Body must be a safe place for layers to be removed and walls to be let down for transparency. You must be an assassin against gossip and teasing in the Student Body. If you find staff spewing gossip, you must act swiftly. The goal is reproduction and you cannot afford the one's helping you to become the abusers of those making themselves ready for reproduction as they stripping away their inhibitions.

Ambiance Principle 3 – You must be "In To Mate"

The point of reproduction is not merely lovemaking. The Student Body cannot be a place for "friends with benefits." Once the friendships move to a commitment, the ones looking for benefits only are out the door. You, your staff, and your student leaders have to be *committed* to position the Student Body for reproduction. You and all of your key leadership have to be into this relationship for the long haul. God illustrates His view on reproduction in a marriage as a blood covenant. I believe this process should be just as serious to us with the Student Body. The Student Body can't just be a one night stand each week for anyone directly placed in it. The Student Body worship service can't be an hour and half "Wham Bam Thank You, Ma'am." The Student Body is committed to God and each other. The sign commitment is preeminent in a Student Body is when you can see trust displayed throughout the Student Body. Trust is displayed when every area of the Student Body knows "Everything you say can, but won't be, held against you."

Ambiance Principle 4 – Deposit the seed
This is where a lot of Student Body worship services and classes miss the mark. The point of reproduction is seed depositing. Every fruit has at least one seed to be redistributed, yet I know of many Student Bodies who are not intentional in releasing the Seed (Word of God) into the Body. Your worship should not take the place of your deposit of Seed. Crowd breakers and fellowship times cannot override the moment for Seed to be deposited. You have created the atmosphere, you have removed the layers, and you have remained committed to the Student Body. But none of these will impregnate. Only the Seed has the potential to make a person reproduce.

At the end of the day, you can't decide the harvest that will be reproduced. This was a revelation to me one day while I was reading Mark 4:4-8.

"As he was scattering the seed, some fell along the path, and the birds came and ate it up. Some fell on rocky places, where it did not have much soil. It sprang up quickly, because the soil was shallow. But when the sun came up, the plants were scorched, and they withered because they had no root. Other seed fell among thorns, which grew up and choked the plants, so that they did not bear grain. Still other seed fell on good soil. It came up, grew and produced a crop, multiplying thirty, sixty, or even a hundred times."

The revelation was that the soil was really the determining factor of what was produced. Beaten down paths have been walked on so long, it's nearly impossible for the Seed to penetrate and reproduce before predators devour it. Hard hearts and rocky situations are almost impossible to reproduce in. Decent soil with too much secular overgrowth will choke the potency out of the Seed as it is growing. Yet, the potential in the Seed never changed despite the soil it was scattered upon. In other words, any potential realized from the seed was determined by the soil it fell upon.

What I am saying is you must be at peace to merely make sure the opportunity is made available each week for the soil to be able to catch the Seed. You have no control over the outcome. Just as a husband and wife cannot control what gender of child they conceive, you will not be able to truly control what type of reproduction goes on in the Student Body. It's the moments of no control and then not really liking the outcome of reproduction in the Student Body that I hold fast to 1 Corinthians 3:6 *"I planted the seed, Apollos watered it, but God made it grow."*

the heart of the matter is...

In my humble opinion, this is a no-brainer. I should not have to tell you what the Heart of the Student Body should be. No, Christ is not the Heart of the matter. Christ's heart for the world should be the Heart of the Student Body. It will be manifested in different ways, but the Great Commission should be the Heart of the Student Body. This Heart pumps Christ's Blood throughout the Student Body. Bottom line, the Student Body's Heart should beat in Morse Code Matthew 28:19-20, "Go and make disciples of all nations, baptizing them in the name of the Father and of the Son and of the Holy Spirit, and teaching them to obey everything I have commanded you."

His mandate for the Student Body is no different today, then the day He spoke it. **Student Bodies today have reduced the Great Commission to a "COME"Mission, when in fact it is a "GO!"Mission.** It will look different for each Student Body. Nevertheless, it is the unifying factor to every denomination, nationality, or creed that believe in the Lord Jesus Christ. Let me break this Go!Mission down for you by bringing to light the action verbs of His Heart for our Student Body.

1. Go! – This is not a "Come"mand.

There is no part of this Heart that has room for us to wait for things to come our way. We are to GO! He never stated where to go, He said GO! He didn't specify for us to remain local or national. He said to GO! If your Student Body is not going, your Student Body's Heart is not beating! I have stopped calling it the Commission from the pulpit, because it starts out with the word "Come." I refuse to let kids think it is okay to just "Come" to our Student Body.

This is so big for me, I made t-shirts a few years back for the conferences which stated, "I Quit Going to Church." You have to get your kids to quit coming to your Student Body and become the living organism that is the Student Body. You do not come to the Student Body. *YOU ARE THE STUDENT BODY AND YOU GO TO THE WORLD!* This is the meaning of Go! And go, we must!

2. Make – Our job does not stop with conversions. It is our Go! Mission to "make" disciples.

As a matter of fact, we are not Christians; we are supposed to be disciples. Semantics? I don't think so. I believe the word "Christian" is thrown around and misused; it has lost its potency. As a matter of fact, the word Christian came about as a slang term to make fun of the Believers of this Gospel. Most Student Bodies fall into one or the other category. They are either evangelistic or they are discipling in their ministry focus. I do not think our Go!Mission provides the choice for either or. We are mandated to make disciples.

Salvation is the ground level of this discipleship process. It boggles my mind how some Student Bodies want to disciple students they never win. It is even more mind-blowing how some Student Bodies want to win students they are never going to disciple. If the Student Body is going to have the Heart of God, we must be intentional in how we make these disciples. Your strategy should be first how you win them to Christ. But do not stop there. You then must be intentional on what the path of a disciple looks like in your Student Body.

3. Baptize – sprinkle, immerse, or take water balloons & water guns to get the job done. Just get the job done.

The reason the church as a whole does not baptize is because we have reduced this gift God left us to a ritual-istic exercise. Baptism IS NOT a ritual. It is supernatural and should be approached that way. Baptism is an outward sign of an inward transformation. I am convinced, the reason we do not see our students die to themselves is because they never drowned themselves in a baptism pool! Baptism is a symbol of the death (down in the water), burial (down under the water), and resurrection (coming up out of the water) of our Lord Jesus Christ went through Himself.

Baptism is a modern day illustration of the Cross. When we do not baptize, we are asking God for His Blood without His Cross. He did not ask us in Luke 9:23 to "deny yourself, take up the blood, and follow me." He said for us to "Take up our cross, daily." When we do not baptize, we are trying to live this faith-walk in flesh form. It is impossible to serve Him and still be alive. My prayer is for a generation to bring a New Holocaust, called water baptism, where every Student

Body is filled with students who die, voluntarily, so they are made alive to their life in Christ.

4. Teach – Instruction can only come from one who has been instructed.

A consistently great teacher is a consistently astute student. Always be one who stays out front in the teaching world by remaining a student yourself. If you stop growing as a student, eventually you will become obsolete as a teacher. It is encouraging to me as a writer that you have made it this far in my book to read this piece. This is a testimony to your commitment to your own personal growth. Let me leave this section with one principle I use when teaching students. It's not enough to have the knowledge. You have to have the moment for imparting that knowledge.

This principle for combining the right moment with the knowledge is what I call, "Planned Spontaneity." I know this is an oxymoron. But I believe there is a powerful principle if you get it. Let me define both words, individually and then merge them for the collective thought.

Planned: to arrange a method or scheme beforehand for (dictionary.com)

Spontaneity: coming or resulting from a natural impulse or tendency (dictionary.com)

As the Mouthpiece, it is imperative for you to have a plan for taking the organization, volunteer staff, and students God put in your ministry through the conflict and issues they are facing. Planning is necessary. Planning is a must. Planning shows your own intentionality and passion for your position in the Student Body. With that said, I do not believe you can force "The Teach." You can cram your directional mission down throats all you care too. But at the end of the day, no individuals or Student Bodies will truly learn and change without hearing the right word in the right moment. This moment is where "Spontaneity" comes into play.

Other books and leadership materials I have read called this a "teachable moment." The premise of a teachable moment is to allow the moment to create the lesson. I love using this method of teaching when it presents itself. My issue is you can't predict the lesson you may teach in any given moment. Planned Spontaneity says, "You control the lesson waiting to be taught as you are looking for the moment to teach it in." In other words, *a teachable moment allows the moment to determine the lesson while planned spontaneity has the lesson waiting for the moment.* The latter seems much more premeditated to me.

The Great Commission is every Student Body's mandate to go, make, baptize, and teach. This is the Heart of God, so why shouldn't it be the Heart of the Student Body. I know it will look different in every Student Body, but I believe you MUST, as the Mouthpiece, ensure that the Student Body remains focused on walking to the Heartbeat of this drum.

the bottom line is...

The prayer I have for this chapter is you will see these areas of the Student Body are the areas that give you distinction from every other Student Body in your area or region. The Goals you reach to attain, whether you reproduce, and the manner in which you seek to fulfill the Great Go!Mission are all areas that make your Student Body unique from any other. I encourage you to not be an idea thief in these areas. If you steal ideas in these areas, you may lose your Student Body's identity. What's the point in that? Spend time in prayer and ask the Holy Spirit to lead you in these areas. These areas are not about a brainstorming session or a whiteboard meeting. These are the identifiers of your Student Body. You must be sensitive to the leading of the Spirit in what Goals He wants your Student Body to attain. Like the Virgin Mary, He wants to "come upon" this Student Body and impregnate you with a destiny and purpose that is beyond your greatest desires. He longs to give you a Divine plan to fulfill His heart for the Great Commission. I'm not going there with you, because He is already there and wants to lead your Student Body to where He is, so you can go there with Him!

— —

I'm Not Fussing!!

➤ Set Goals! Who wants to be a part of something that has no ambition to go any further than what they already are? Need I say more?

➤ Atmosphere is key in getting the Student Body open to receive seed.

➤ Be a thermometer. It is your job to read the temperature of the room. You have to always be checking the atmosphere in the Student Body.

➤ Be a thermostat. Once you have read the atmosphere of the room, it is now your job to get it where it needs to be to make ready for impartation.

➤ Don't force the seed of God into the Student Body if the atmosphere is not right. Forced penetration is called rape. There is way too much of this going on in Student Bodies across the world. I will leave this right there.

➤ Decide what the Great Go!Mission looks like for your Student Body.

➤ Outreach is defined as meeting the needs of the community. Everyone can do the Great Go!Mission. Find a need and begin filling it.

What You Need To Do is...

➤ Spend 1 Monday analyzing where the Student Body is in 5 strategic areas of ministry. (Worship, Ministry, Evangelism, Discipleship, Fellowship)

➢ Spend the following Monday setting 3 achievable goals for each of the 5 areas that are quantifiable and you can be held accountable to fulfill within the next 12 months. These goals MUST be for the forward progress of the Student Body

➢ Create 3 multi-sensory worship services that are beyond what the normal youth service looks like.

➢ Evaluate why you go to certain camps versus others and certain conferences versus others. Camps, conferences and Fests should all go back to giving you tools to create atmosphere.

➢ You should personally go on a mission trip before you endeavor to take your students.

➢ Create local missions projects that the Student Body can do to make a difference around the community.

➢ Sponsor 1 child as a group for Feed the Children.

➢ Work towards local, national, and international mission's trips.

➢ Begin speaking to the heart of the missionaries that are connected to the Student Body and do not even realize they are called.

➢ Give "high challenge" messages about the need for Reformers in this generation.

➢ BAPTIZE!

Chapter 12

Getting Comfortable in Your New Skin

*"...pour new wine into new wineskins,
and both are preserved."*
Matthew 9:17

Oh the late 90's...

When my wife and I graduated Bible College in 1999, I never dreamed I would only serve as the Mouthpiece for one Student Body, at one church, serving under one Head. I was a volunteer youth staff member while in college, and I even did an interim pastorate while the church transitioned from one youth pastor to another. So my entire Student Body experience rests at one location with one Head. Before you discredit me as a source for understanding the real Student Body culture, let me validate myself.

I have spent well over a decade listening to my peers brag about how they go into new places and basically do a "new and improved" version of the youth ministry they did at their previous church. The latest stat on youth pastor longevity at one Student Body was 18 months. The thought of building 78 sermons, scheduling 18 events, preparing for 6 staff meetings, and developing a discipleship system that will only last 18 months is very appealing to me in theory. I am absolutely convinced I could be a master at Angry Birds, Plants versus Zombies, Doodle Jump, and Risk on my iPhone.

In contrast to being a part of one Student Body for only 18 months, I have had to continually re-invent my teaching methods, my sermon delivery, the way I approach staff development, and especially how I create points of connections for potentially new members of the Student Body. Let me walk down memory lane with you for a moment as I reminisce about how my Student Body has changed from 1996 until now.

-mobile phones moved from the bags doctors, lawyers, and drug dealers carried to the device that only weird and irrelevant people lack

-text messaging became the primary method of information transfer versus just talking on the phone

-computers moved from being in a room tied to a cable modem to being as mobile as an iPad the size of a paper notebook.

-mid week services transitioned from being an entire church congregation to full blown services individualized for specific age groups.

-church sanctuaries moved from overhead projectors with transparencies to HD video projection with lyrics on top of video backgrounds.

-churches moved from Hymnals & Convention Songs to Praise & Worship and now moving back to Hymnals

-The Student Body moved from being babysitting, pizza parties and afterglows to serious discipleship training and development of students at this crucial stage of development.

What I think is amazing is the fact that I have had the joy of transitioning one Student Body through all of these stages of development. Others had to pick up where their predecessors had left off, while my staff and I have been a consistent catalyst for change during these evolutions of information and technology. It has been an absolute joy of mine to walk with the same Student Body on this journey. Yet, none of these can hold a candle to the two greatest joys of my ministry thus far.

Greatest Joy #1: Watching my 1st group of 6th graders graduate from college.

The majority of youth pastors never see their 6th graders graduate Junior High. I have had the joy of watching my students' graduate college every year since 2008. I will never forget the day I sat watching my very first student walk across the stage to shake the hand of the president of the university. It was a moment I will cherish for a lifetime. She came into the Student Body a cute, homely, little baby and has now blossomed into a strong, beautiful woman on the brink of getting married in just a few short weeks.

My wife and I pulled her and three other students from that first group of graduates into one of our education classrooms and gave each of them a ring with a ruby stone in it. As I placed the ring on their fingers, I quoted Proverbs 31. I declared their value to be FAR above rubies. As Em and I hugged each of the four, we all wept uncontrollably. The students had no idea why this was such a big deal. Truth is, they were probably crying because we were. But for Em and I, this was a zenith in our Student Body commitment that we knew was more special than just abandoning ship when things were difficult.

Greatest Joy #2: Having a child of one of my former youth members now be a part of the Student Body I lead.

In our Family Life Center foyer hangs a poster rack like what you would see at K-Mart or Wal-Mart to display all the posters you could purchase. I was on vacation and noticed a K-Mart going out of business, so I went in and spoke directly to the manager about the poster display he had. I played the "lowly youth pastor" card really well. SO well in fact, he gave it to me for free. I mounted the display in the foyer and we place pictures of each year of ministry on one poster page that you can flip through. It has been amazing to see grown men and women in our church come to the poster rack and show their kids what they use to look like when they were in the youth group. The reason I say, "Youth Group" is because that was what it was back in the day.

The strangest and greatest thing was when I saw one of my young 6th graders standing by the poster rack trying to find her mom at the front of the rack. Before you think I am a relic, her mom got pregnant in high school. It was a hard journey for this mom. Even today, the struggles of her past come into play in her daughter's life. But one of my greatest joys is to now be ministering to this one family in a generational way. The joy I feel isn't so much about being in youth ministry so long, as it about being in ONE Student Body so long that I get to lead one of my former students as a parent to one of my current students. I'm not sure, but I cannot recall any youth pastors I am affiliated with that has accomplished the feat of being the Mouthpiece for one Student Body at one church long enough to minister to a former youth member's child.

The question I ask is, "WHY?" Why is it that the average Student Pastor can only stay for 18 months?

The answer I get is one of these two answers.

1. Being a Mouthpiece for a Student Body is a stepping stone to being your own Head

2. Being in the Student Body is too frustrating to be in
long term.

Unless you are just a selfish jerk, answer number 2 is most
likely the answer. Yep, I said it. I am convinced, the reason
most people get out of the Student Body is because you have
not clearly understood the cycle of Student Ministry. You
will constantly live frustrated if you do not understand that
the Student Body sheds its skin.

Shedding of the Skin
According to an article I read on WebMD, the average
body sheds its skin and even shifts its chemistry every 5-7
years. Another article went on to say that the average body
loses almost 1.5 pounds of skin a year. That is well over 40
pounds of skin shedding in a lifetime. In other words, the
human body is in a constant state of metamorphosis. The
skin you have today will not be there 5 years from now. It
sheds. Just like the human body, the Student Body is in a
cycle of change as well.

This constant state of shedding skin is the root cause of
frustration for most Mouthpieces I know. The endless cycle
of students in and out of the Student Body can be extremely
frustrating. You grow those Vacation Bible School babies
into know-it-all teenagers until they get that "ah-ha" moment
and begin to mature into young disciples of Christ. By the
time they become something you can work with, they either
leave for college or join the choir! Trust me; I know how
frustrating it can be when you do not understand the Student
Body was meant to shed its skin.

What you have to understand is kids were never meant
to stay kids! Ask the senior adult mom, who still has her 45
year old son living with her, if there are things she wished
she would have done differently with him. Ask the husband
of an extremely high maintenance wife, because she wants

him to be as lavish as her daddy was, if he could go back and change his plea of "for better or worse." Next time you go to your local high school football game, look around and see the 25 year olds still wearing their high school letter jackets (which is 3 sizes too small because of their beer belly) from their "glory days" because they never grew beyond the high school mentality. The same is true in the church world. If we in the Student Body aren't careful, we will have an old and odd student ministry.

Your attendance may be great, but your effectiveness in maintaining the Student Body may be absolutely horrendous. At the end of the day, there may be some skin that needs to peel and unnecessary weight to shed.

Just like the human body, the Student Body should maintain a 5-7 year shedding cycle as well. Think about it. If you get a student in 6th or 7th grade and they run with you until 1 or 2 years into their college life, you should see yourself as operating a successful Student Body. There will be some cases where development of those students did not take place as it should have. In those RARE cases, you may leave a student in until they graduate college in a 4 year situation. However, NO persons beyond a 4 year degree should be in the Student Body unless you call them staff, or a student calls them "mom or dad." Otherwise, you are getting your Student Body out of shape. Let me put it another way, *as irrelevant as the Student Body should be to a 3rd grader is as irrelevant as it should be to a junior in college*. I have had so many of my peers use the motto, "It's about butts in the seats." In reference to chapter 7 you will have a surplus if you're not shedding.

You are a seed planter. You do not determine the soil, nor do you provide the water or increase. Since God created the Student Body and He is the ultimate authority over the blessing, favor, and anointing to pour down it, you have to be at peace to shed every 5-7 years. Why? God fashioned it to be this way. God has an agenda for each person greater than what you and I can imagine or create. The tendency for us is to use our position in a student's life to unintentionally guilt them into remaining immature. I hear parents complaining at almost every graduation ceremony I go too, "I wish I could go back and do it all over. There are so many things I would change." My friend, you and I have a mulligan every 5-7 years. The skin changes, but the structure and alignment must always stay the same. We get "do-over's."

Please pay attention in the "I'm not fussing" and the "What you need to do" section of this chapter. I will give you some practical help for keeping the shedding of skin a positive thing for your Student Body.

— —

I'm Not Fussing!!

➢ Take a quick inventory.

-How many people come to your Student Body that are out of high school?

-How many of those people are not on your volunteer staff?

-How many people out of high school are on your YOUTH praise team or drama team?

➢ Celebrate transitions. Growth is the whole point of discipleship. Great leadership is constantly keeping "what's next" in front.

➢ Grieve, but do not regret the shedding of skin. You should be sad. It should make a small hole in your heart. But you can't die and want to quit because your favorites move beyond you. They will be okay and so will the Student Body.

➢ When you start sensing a new cycle coming, start investing in the new babies coming in. This will make the shedding of the old skin easier to handle in your heart.

What You Need To Do is...
- ➢ Find a way to develop a graduating worship band. This is really simple if you have an individual Middle school, High school, and college worship service.
- ➢ Do the same for drama teams and every other possible ministry opportunity. Again, if you have individual breaks for Middle – College, this is simple. If not, I would strongly encourage you to begin setting the breaks into motion. Logistics can be a nightmare, but it will be HUGE for you in the long run.
- ➢ Create a "Rite of passage" for the students that shed off the Student Body. Raising a Modern Day Knight by Robert Lewis really brought home this concept to me. Because of this book we now do 3 very effective rites of passages for the Student Body.
  1. Graduation Sunday – Before you tune me out, listen. Instead of celebrating High school and college grads we honor those who graduate at every significant stage. Preschool to Elementry school, 5th grade to Middle school, Middle school to High school, and then the High school and college grads all get honored on that Sunday. We honor each transition group with a transition Bible. By Transition Bible, I mean a Bible my Head, my inner 3, and I have agreed upon for each stage in development. Email me if you want to know the Bibles we use.
  2. Back to School Blessing – The Sunday before every new school year, we anoint with oil and pray over every family, every student, and every teaching professional. It's a monumental day. It is

also, one of the highest attended Sunday morning services of the year!

3. Midnight Communion – I got this concept from a pioneer in youth ministry named Jeanne Mayo. All credit belongs to her. Bottom line: I make a significant night just for my high school grads, my wife, my college pastor, and I to be alone together to celebrate. We do several spiritual things that end with taking Holy Communion together. But I sandwich those things with a ton of fun activities that I pay for, as my graduation gift to them. It usually goes from 8pm-3am. We end the night with toilet papering someone's house who is in our church. Now before you start quoting previous chapters at me, I call the people to let them know we are coming, and not to shoot and that I will come back by the next morning and clean up the yard. The grads don't know it, so it's fun for them!

Conclusion

Come Together Right Now...

"not forsaking our own assembling together,
as is the habit of some..."
Hebrews 10:25

I am a huge fan of old music. I don't know what it is, but "today's music ain't got the same soul" or something. Not only do I love old music, but my son and two of my nephews are HUGE Beatles fans. As I was riding down the road surfing through radio stations, I came across the old Beatles tune, "Come Together," Now I have to admit, as soon as I heard the song come on, I rolled the windows down and pulled my sunroof back in my tan Jeep Commander so I could blast this "REAL" music for all those I passed by to hear when my Hemi engine wasn't roaring. Yea, I'm one of those guys. Luckily, I did not have my shirt unbuttoned so my chest hair and gold necklace could show! Haha (That's funny right there.) It was so fun hearing this song as I am driving back to the office to conclude this book. To be honest, I am listening to this song via my iTunes account even now while I am typing. It's such a cool groove song. Just so I can get you in the moment, let me quote a few lyrics to get you in the mood to end this book and set you on your journey to align the Student Body you serve as the Mouthpiece for.

Here come old flattop, he come grooving up slowly
He got joo-joo eyeball, he one holy roller
He got hair down to his knee
Got to be a joker he just do what he please

He wear no shoeshine, he got toe-jam football
He got monkey finger, he shoot coca-cola
He say "I know you, you know me"
One thing I can tell you is you got to be free
Come together right now over me

He bag production, he got walrus gumboot
He got Ono sideboard, he one spinal cracker
He got feet down below his knee
Hold you in his armchair you can feel his disease
Come together right now over me

He roller-coaster, he got early warning
He got muddy water, he one mojo filter
He say "One and one and one is three"
Got to be good-looking cause he's so hard to see
Come together right now over me

Come together
Yeah come together
Yeah come together...
(Lennon/McCartney)

This is a great song, huh?

No. I have no idea what these guys are saying. I am looking at these words while hearing the song and still can't figure out what in the world they are trying to communicate. Is it about the war? Is it about the drugs they obviously are on? Is it about Peace, Love & Rock n Roll? What in the world are they saying? I am terrified to know what a "walrus gumboot" is. I am laughing a little as I reflect back on my ride back to the office. I realized, I was not singing this song at all. Truth is, I know 6 words of this entire song by heart, "Come together right now, over me." But only four of those words make any sense to me in terms of a complete thought. How do you come together right now over me exactly? As I sit here typing, I am realizing that is exactly why this book is so important for me to write. Truth is we have only been singing the part of alignment we know. The whole truth is, we make no sense at all to any other part of the Student Body but we want them to "come together right now." We sound like we are on drugs to them, because we talk about this and that. We make fun of this person and that person. We cry "poor mouth" to this person. We gossip about our Head to deacons and council members. We sit around making plans about our exit strategy. All the while, we want the entire Student Body to "come together right now." I don't think so. The reason is because we don't understand what demons do about placement.

demons don't fight each other...

Even demons understand alignment. There is nowhere in Scripture where you will ever see demons or witches or any type of demonic influence at war within their own ranks. The principalities of this world understand where they fit in their body. They are not disorganized nor are they operating in chaos. As a matter of fact, the chaos they seek to incite in the lives of Believers is very intentional and strategic. See the alignment in this verse:

"When he saw Jesus from a distance, he ran and fell on his knees in front of him. He shouted at the top of his voice, "What do you want with me, Jesus, Son of the Most High God? Swear to God that you won't torture me!" For Jesus had said to him, "Come out of this man, you evil spirit!"

Then Jesus asked him, "What is your name?" "My name is Legion," he replied, "for we are many." And he begged Jesus again and again not to send them out of the area." (Mark 5:6-10)

Notice how Jesus asked for the name of a singular spirit, yet they responded to Him united as one group of many. The word, "Legion" refers to a regimented, militant group who march together as one. Satan's body is fully aware of ranks and operates under that alignment. There are no rogue demons out doing there own thing. You haven't heard of one demon trying to earn its graces back into heaven's ranks. They are walking in sync with the orders given to them.

Also notice how they begged Christ to not "send them out of the area." The implication is this Legion was assigned to a specific location on the earth. They were assigned to remain in this particular territory. Staying possessed in the man was not the greatest priority. They would hang out in pigs if it was necessary, but they did not want to abandon their assigned territory. They were committed. They were determined to stay at their post. There was no bickering or back-biting or jockeying for position. They knew they were collectively assigned and wanted to remain in their position. If you haven't picked up on it, Satan's minions are highly organized, effective, and united.

Check this passage out.

[24] But when the Pharisees heard this, they said, "It is only by Beelzebul, the prince of demons that this fellow drives out demons." Jesus knew their thoughts and said to them, "Every kingdom divided against itself will be ruined, and every city or household divided against itself will not stand. [26] If Satan drives out Satan, he is divided against himself. How then can his kingdom stand? [27] And if I drive out demons by Beelzebul, by whom do your people drive them

out? So then, they will be your judges. [28] But if it is by the Spirit of God that I drive out demons, then the kingdom of God has come upon you. (Matthew 12:24-28)

Jesus makes it very clear that Satan's kingdom is not divided. There is an alignment in his body that is not separated in agenda or practice. We quote from this passage often. What is interesting to me is we have no idea what the context is for the quote we use. Even Christ, Himself, is declaring Satan's body united and undivided. You won't find a passage where you see demons fighting each other for position or territory. You will never hear or read where a demon is trying to overthrow Satan's rule. You are not going to read about demons starting their own work or starting their own DEMONATIONS. There is no account of a council trying to have another demon deacon removed from the board. No story about certain states ready to become independent because their tithe of tithes is unfair. Nope. None of this stuff happens in the ranks of Hell, we keep all of this for the church!

It's only in church where you find preachers fighting other preachers. It's only in church where you see deacons coming against elders. It's the church where you find Baptists tearing down Methodists, and Methodists tearing down Pentecostals, and Pentecostals tearing down Charismatic's, and Charismatic's fighting the Presbyterians. Why? The reason the Body of Christ fights is because we do not understand alignment. We have to get some order in the House of God. An Awakening of Alignment must come to the Body of Believers. We have to expel every chaotic, renegade spirit from the Body of Christ. Chaos is a work of the enemy. "God is not the author of confusion, so let everything be done decently and in order." At some point you and I are going to have to stop singing, "come together right now" and start demanding alignment or they need to get out. It's time for us to stop all this nonsense we try to call church and get in alignment for what the House of God is trying to accomplish. "As for me and my house we will" has to become our battle cry. Why? Because we are after a commanded blessing for the Student Body.

alignment + oil at the Feet = the commanded blessing

Simply, your job is alignment. You, Mouthpiece, have to have a fierce commitment to alignment. You can't live with mediocrity and half-hearted commitment. What you are after is too important and too necessary for the sustaining of the Student Body to just let things slide. *You are after a commanded blessing that does not come from suggested unity.* There is no time for you to be passive. There is no time for you to sit around and wait for your senior pastor role, before you will make changes. You can't afford for the opinions of people to dictate your ability to confront insubordination. There is no time for you to live intimidated and insecure. You are after a commanded blessing this world has yet to see. This earth is groaning for the redeemed ones to rise and take their place in the earth. You must fight for alignment. It's too important to allow the Student Body to live as a paraplegic.

Any Body with no head is dead from the start. Get clear on who is the head of the Student Body and insure that everyone under this headship knows whom they are looking to for the signals of the Student Body. No matter how you feel about the person in the position, keep taking your signals. Take what he/she signals to you and rally the body to "Come together, UNDER you."

Any Body that cannot speak is a mute. You must speak, so speak life into dead allegiance. You may have very well been the point where poison penetrated the Student Body. It's okay. Fix it and let healing come to the sick areas through your words. You keep speaking and watch it "Come together."

Allow your inner 3 and volunteer staff to function as only they can. They will not do it just like you. They may not handle situations just the way you would want, and that's okay. If God wanted you to do everything He would have made you with clones! Release responsibility and watch the oil flow down!

Create in your Belly hunger pains for His presence. Find ways to get them hungry. Not your whole group, just your core needs strengthening. If you fix your core, everywhere else gets healthier as well. Get the Belly firm and watch "rivers of living water flow." Keep your core students aligned and watch how easy it is for the rest of the Student Body to "Come together."

The Student Body Legs were meant to create movement. The Student Body is not lame. The Student Body needs no crutches or a cane. There is no need to limp along through middle school and high school years. If the Student Body is limping along, find a way to make the adjustments to get them to "Come together right now."

The Student Body Feet provides the traction to get the Body progressing. You may have no traction. You may feel like you have clubbed feet. I want you to know that the Giver of the blessing, favor and anointing can heal feet which seem to be withered. He is no respecter of Student Bodies. What He has done for others, He has the power to do for you. Your situation is not so bad, your leadership skills are not so poor, and your budget is not so small that God cannot command a blessing to hit your Student Body.

I declare to you today is the beginning of a new dawn for your Student Body. You can make it aligned. You will have the leadership to straighten things up. You will find the resources. You won't have to beg and plead for favor. It is coming to your Student Body. Why? A COMMANDED BLESSING is flowing your way. You don't control the flow of the oil. You have no say in what type of blessing gets commanded. You are not responsible for the timing. All you have to focus on is the alignment of the Student Body. Don't get distracted. Don't allow yourself to be "MAN"ipulated. Be GOD-ipulated. Focus on staying in alignment. When you see a part of the Student Body getting out, be a spiritual chiropractor and make the necessary adjustment. Carry your hammer and bust every dam in the Student Body. Be bold and courageous enough to not allow mutiny in the Body and you, my friend, will experience a blessing that "eye has not seen and ear has not heard." All because you were in the right place to position the entire Student Body for a commanded blessing God is excited to pour down the Student Body.

I pray I have helped.

CPSIA information can be obtained at www.ICGtesting.com
Printed in the USA
LVOW061347031111

253377LV00001B/146/P